Cambridge Elements ≡

Elements in Magic
edited by
Marion Gibson
University of Exeter

REPRESENTING MAGIC IN MODERN IRELAND

Belief, History, and Culture

Andrew Sneddon
Ulster University

CAMBRIDGE
UNIVERSITY PRESS

CAMBRIDGE
UNIVERSITY PRESS

University Printing House, Cambridge CB2 8BS, United Kingdom

One Liberty Plaza, 20th Floor, New York, NY 10006, USA

477 Williamstown Road, Port Melbourne, VIC 3207, Australia

314–321, 3rd Floor, Plot 3, Splendor Forum, Jasola District Centre,
New Delhi – 110025, India

103 Penang Road, #05–06/07, Visioncrest Commercial, Singapore 238467

Cambridge University Press is part of the University of Cambridge.

It furthers the University's mission by disseminating knowledge in the pursuit of
education, learning, and research at the highest international levels of excellence.

www.cambridge.org
Information on this title: www.cambridge.org/9781108949279
DOI: 10.1017/9781108954044

© Andrew Sneddon 2022

First published 2022

A catalogue record for this publication is available from the British Library.

ISBN 978-1-108-94927-9 Paperback
ISSN 2732-4087 (online)
ISSN 2732-4079 (print)

Cambridge University Press has no responsibility for the persistence or accuracy of
URLs for external or third-party internet websites referred to in this publication
and does not guarantee that any content on such websites is, or will remain,
accurate or appropriate.

Representing Magic in Modern Ireland

Belief, History, and Culture

Elements in Magic

DOI: 10.1017/9781108954044
First published online: April 2022

Andrew Sneddon
Ulster University

Author for correspondence: Dr Andrew Sneddon, a.sneddon@ulster.ac.uk

Abstract: This Element argues that Ireland did not experience a disenchanted modernity, nor a decline in magic. It suggests that beliefs, practices, and traditions concerning witchcraft and magic developed and adapted to modernity to retain cultural currency until the end of the twentieth century. This analysis provides the backdrop for the first systematic exploration of how historic Irish trials of witches and cunning folk were represented by historians, antiquarians, journalists, dramatists, poets, and novelists in Ireland between the late eighteenth and late twentieth centuries. It is demonstrated that this work created an accepted narrative of Irish witchcraft and magic that glossed over, ignored, or obscured the depth of belief in witchcraft, both in the past and in contemporary society. Collectively, their work gendered Irish witchcraft, created a myth of a disenchanted, modern Ireland, and reinforced competing views of Irishness and Irish identity. These long-held stereotypes were only challenged in the late twentieth century.

Keywords: modernity, witchcraft, magic, Ireland, decline

ISBNs: 9781108949279 (PB), 9781108954044 (OC)
ISSNs: 2732-4087 (online), 2732-4079 (print)

Contents

1 Introduction

'Modernity' is an ambiguous concept that 'has come to signify a mixture of political, social, intellectual, economic, technological, and psychological factors'. These factors include 'the emergence of the autonomous and rational subject; the differentiation of cultural spheres; the rise of liberal and democratic states; the turn to psychologism and self-reflexivity; and the dominance of secularism, nationalism, capitalism, industrialism, urbanism, consumerism, and scientism'.[1] Modernity is also often conceptualised as 'disenchanted'. In its broadest definition, 'disenchantment' maintains 'that wonders and marvels have been demystified by science, spirituality has been supplanted by secularism, spontaneity has been replaced by bureaucratization, and the imagination has been subordinated to instrumental reason'.[2] The Protestant Reformation is often regarded as a landmark moment in European disenchantment when religious reformers eliminated key assumptions about the intervention of immaterial, magical, and supernatural forces in the universe. This religious revolution was regarded as a stop on the way to the Enlightenment of the eighteenth century, which marked an even greater triumph of rationality over ignorance and superstition.[3] When sociologist Max Weber appropriated the phrase 'the disenchantment of the world' from Friedrich Schiller in the early twentieth century, he created a way of looking at modernity and its relationship with enchantment (including the perceived decline of magical culture) that historians, sociologists, and philosophers have only (fairly) recently begun to problematise and challenge.[4]

In the past three decades or so, historians have increasingly argued that there was no decline in magic, or indeed an eclipse of belief in a moral and magical universe, in western Europe, including Britain, during the Enlightenment. It has been demonstrated that widespread belief in witchcraft and fear of witches continued after the end of European witch-hunting in the late eighteenth century, up until at least the early twentieth century. The harmful magic of witches continued to be fought using a wide array of anti-witch measures, ranging from protective or apotropaic magic to simple incantations and rituals to the more complicated counter-magic of skilled practitioners. Suspected witches were also threatened verbally and (often violently) attacked by individuals or mobs.[5] Historians increasingly find it difficult to maintain that

---

[1] Saler, 'Modernity and Enchantment', p. 694.   [2] Saler, 'Modernity and Enchantment', p. 692.
[3] Walsham, 'Disenchantment', p. 497.
[4] See Jenkins, 'Disenchantment, Enchantment and Re-Enchantment', pp. 11–32; Storm, *Myth of Disenchantment*; Meyer and Pels, *Magic and Modernity*.
[5] See, Davies, *Witchcraft, Magic and Culture*; Davies, *America Bewitched*; Davies, 'Reverse Witch Trials'; Davies and de Blécourt, *Beyond the Witch Trials*; Davies and de Blécourt, *Witchcraft*

scepticism and belief in witchcraft and magic were binaries that inevitably replaced one another, arguing instead that they often shared the same intellectual and mental space and worked to mutually reinforce one another.[6] Karl Bell has recently adopted an 'alternative conceptualisation of adaption and transformed continuation' to challenge this traditional, magic/modernity dichotomy. Magical beliefs and practices are shown to have enabled people in Victorian Britain, from a variety of socio-economic backgrounds, even those living in towns and cities, to negotiate the challenges and uncertainties of modernity. Bell's model of adaptive, transformative continuation rejects the 'Weberian paradigm' while avoiding 'the false breakages that accompany the enchantment/disenchantment/re-enchantment trichotomy'.[7] This trichotomy is often seen to comprise three stages of magical evolution: an enchanted medieval and early modern period, where belief in magic and witchcraft was widespread; a period of decline in magic and witchcraft in the late seventeenth and early eighteenth centuries; and a re-enchantment of elite culture, marked by occult revivals in the late eighteenth and late nineteenth centuries. This trichotomy is able to incorporate a continuation of magical belief and behaviour among ordinary people when it suggests that decline and re-enchantment chiefly affected literate elites.[8] Thomas Waters has employed a similar approach to Bell in his study of witchcraft and harmful magic in nineteenth- and twentieth-century Britain, arguing that 'Throughout its long history, witchcraft has always altered and developed. But it has been particularly mutable during the last two hundred years, as the pace of cultural and social change has quickened.'[9] He has shown that witchcraft was believed in, feared, and fought by individuals, mobs, and unwitchers (notably cunning folk and fortune tellers) across Britain, throughout the nineteenth century. Cunning folk were magical practitioners who provided a wide range of services – including divination, love magic,

---

Continued; Henderson, *Witchcraft and Folk Belief*; Tallis, 'Which Craft?'; Waters, 'Belief in Witchcraft in Oxfordshire and Warwickshire', pp. 103–5; Hutton, 'Manx Witchcraft'; Suggett, *Magic and Witchcraft*, pp. 128–33, 142–54.

[6] Clark, *Thinking with Demons*, pp. 195–213; Gaskill, *Crime and Mentalities*, pp. 188–9; Taussig, 'Viscerality, Faith and Scepticism'.

[7] Bell, *Magical Imagination*, p. 79.

[8] A good example of the trichotomy model, which discusses re-enchantment in relation to the revival of occult thinking among British literate elites in the late eighteenth century: Monod, *Solomon's Secret Arts*. For a recent articulation of the view that a decline of magic occurred in eighteenth-century Britain, among male elites, if not the population as large: Hunter, *Decline of Magic*. For the occult revival of the later Victorian period (an era also marked by secularisation and increasing prominence of scientific naturalism), which saw the rise of spiritualism, psychical research, theosophy, and the establishment of secret magical societies, such as the Hermetic Order of the Golden Dawn: Waters, *Cursed Britain*, pp. 139–55; Owen, *Place of Enchantment*; Owen, *Darkened Room*; Leeder, *Modern Supernatural*; Butler, *Victorian Occultism*.

[9] Waters, *Cursed Britain*, p. 262.

and the detection, countering, and curing of witchcraft – for a small fee or payment in kind. While, in the late nineteenth century, the avant-garde elite of the Victorian occult revival increasingly explored the existence of supernatural harm and healing, and British colonisers returned home from Africa, India, and the Caribbean less dismissive of the power of witchcraft and magic.[10]

This new-found respect for the magical beliefs of indigenous cultures should not be overplayed. In the nineteenth and (for much of the) twentieth centuries, anthropologists used magic to distinguish modern Western rationality from the 'primitive' or 'savage' 'other', 'by exposing the backwardness or delusions of shamanism, fetishism, magic and witchcraft'.[11] According to Waters, the early to mid-twentieth century witnessed 'witchcraft's decline' in Britain 'from a majority belief to a fringe credo'. This was largely the result of cultural changes, including a decline in oral storytelling, a downturn in popular Christianity, and the fact that witchcraft lost its raison d'être to explain and help people cope with uncertainty and misfortune in the 'increasingly comfortable and less dangerous' world created 'by the growth of the welfare state and massive advances in scientific medicine'. The primary reason, however, given for the collapse of witchcraft was that 'the British state used regulation to eliminate the cunning-craft, the ancient trade of the white witches, who had previously propagated this belief system'. Belief in harmful witchcraft however revived in the liberal environment of late twentieth-century multicultural Britain.[12] Witchcraft in this period 'developed in ways that brought them more into line with the changing intellectual climate and new regulatory structures ... an example of maleficent witchcraft's acculturalization or modernization'. For example, 'some hues of witchcraft belief incorporated thoroughly modern pseudo-scientific and psychological terminology into their conceptual vocabulary', while 'others developed new, more religious, and ultimately more law-abiding counter-witchcraft therapies'.[13]

This Element charts belief in witchcraft and magic in Ireland beyond the point at which previous studies stopped, in the early 1920s,[14] when Ireland was partitioned and the new jurisdictions of the Irish Free State (which became the Republic of Ireland in 1949 and comprised twenty-six counties) and Northern

---

[10] Waters, *Cursed Britain*, pp. 9–187 (quote at p. 262).

[11] Pels, 'Introduction: Magic and Modernity', p. 6.

[12] Waters, *Cursed Britain*, pp. 187–260 (quotes at pp. 262, 263).

[13] Waters, 'Maleficent Witchcraft', pp. 117–8. For more on maleficent witchcraft and magic in twentieth-century Britain: Davies, *Witchcraft, Magic and Culture*; Davies, *Supernatural War*; Davies, 'Reverse Witch Trials'.

[14] See Fulton, 'Clerics, Conjurors and Courtrooms'; Sneddon and Fulton, 'Witchcraft'; Sneddon, *Witchcraft and Magic in Ireland*.

Ireland (containing six counties in the province of Ulster) were created. It demonstrates that modern Ireland was neither 'disenchanted', nor did it experience a decline in belief in witchcraft and magic. It suggests that the British model of adaptive, transformative continuation is also applicable to Ireland. Irish belief in witchcraft and popular magic in the nineteenth and twentieth centuries was nevertheless distinct from that of Britain and evolved in different ways and at a different rate of change. In doing so, this Element acts as a further corrective to the once pervasive practice of excluding the Irish experience from summaries of witchcraft and magic in early modern and modern Europe. In doing so, an incredibly rich body of source material, from official documents, pamphlets, folklore to literature and historical writing, has been overlooked.

This Element also provides the first analysis of Irish historical writing on witchcraft and suggests it represents an important but overlooked part of the wider historiography of the subject. Through a systematic exploration of the ways in which Irish historians interpreted salient, historic cases of witchcraft and magic, it is argued that Irish witchcraft historiography began in the early nineteenth century and comprised published transcriptions of original documents as well as interpretative narrative histories. This latter work may have lacked the standards of presentation or historical contextualisation of the academic histories of Irish witchcraft that first appeared in the 1990s but was nevertheless based on primary-source evidence; in many cases, on the original documents that demonologists, antiquarians, and local historians had made widely available from the late seventeenth century onwards. This historiography (which was still being written up until the early 2000s) has been incredibly influential in shaping wider perceptions of Irish witchcraft and magic. Influenced by the Enlightenment rhetoric of Protestants of the Anglican Ascendancy in the eighteenth century, Irish historians of witchcraft distanced themselves from early modern witch-hunting in a particular way, through Irish exceptionalism: Irish witch trials were regarded as aberrations, occurring in a largely witchcraft-free country. This idea of a largely disenchanted past was matched to a disenchanted present, and the fact that many people still believed in witchcraft in modern Ireland was overlooked, denied or ignored. These histories also gendered witchcraft as female to articulate and maintain gender norms. This picture of Irish witchcraft first painted by nineteenth-century historians was weaponised and taken to a wider audience by nineteenth- and twentieth-century journalists. Irish witchcraft was gendered to an even greater extent and used to articulate politically and culturally nuanced views of Irish identity. This reimagining of Irish witchcraft occurred against a backdrop of war and political crisis, when the map of Ireland was redrawn and Irish identity refashioned. In the twentieth century, Irish dramatists, poets, and novelists were influenced by this historical writing and often incorporated published primary sources in their work. The gendering and politicisation of Irish witchcraft trials were challenged in the very late twentieth century by historians, artists, and creative writers willing to break age-long stereotypes of the Irish witch figure.

The Witchcraft Cases

Irish representations of witchcraft and magic (by historians, artists, journalists, and creative writers) studied in this Element are viewed through the lens of three principal trials and prosecutions: the trial and conviction for witchcraft of Florence Newton in 1661 in County Cork; the trials of the 'Islandmagee witches' in County Antrim in 1711; and the prosecution of Mary Butters (the 'Carnmoney witch') for murder in 1808. Butters was an infamous magical practitioner who specialised in curing bewitched cattle and fortune telling. Two other Irish cases are touched upon but are not dealt with in as much detail. The first of these took place in Antrim town, County Antrim, in 1698, when a nine-year-old girl accused an elderly woman of her bewitchment by means of demonic possession. Traditionally regarded as a witch trial by historians and folklorists,[15] this case was in fact an extrajudicial killing: the nameless old woman in question was apprehended, strangled, and burned by her neighbours without due legal process being followed.[16] The second case occurred in Kilkenny in 1324, two centuries before malefic witchcraft became a crime in Ireland. It centred on the politically motivated prosecution of Anglo-Irish elite colonists, Alice Kyteler and her associates, for heresy, demonic conspiracy, and the use of harmful magic by Richard de Ledrede, English Franciscan Bishop of Ossory. Kyteler evaded arrest by fleeing to England and was tried and convicted in absentia. Her co-conspirators were banished, flogged, or excommunicated, while Petronella de Midia was tortured and burned alive.[17]

Florence Newton, Cork, 1661

Sixty-five-year-old Florence Newton, from Youghal, County Cork, was convicted of witchcraft in Autumn 1661.[18] At that time, the English settler port town of

---

[15] Seymour, *Irish Witchcraft and Demonology*, pp. 194–8; Lapoint, 'Irish Immunity', p. 77; Croker, 'Witchcraft in Kilkenny', p. 341.

[16] Sneddon, 'Medicine, Belief, Witchcraft', pp. 81–6.

[17] Sneddon, *Witchcraft and Magic in Ireland*, pp. 16–17, 71, 112; Sneddon, 'Templars, the Witch, and the Wild Irish (Review)'; Goodare, *European Witch-hunt*, pp. 38–9; Lapoint, 'Irish Immunity', p. 78. Some historians have argued that the Kyteler case was the first European witchcraft trial: Riddell, 'First Execution for Witchcraft in Ireland'; Callan, *Templars, the Witch, and the Wild Irish*, pp. 77–148.

[18] The following description of events leading up to and during the trial of Newton is based on: Sneddon, 'Florence Newton's Trial', pp. 298–319. For more on Newton's trial: McAuliffe,

Youghal contained around 2,300 inhabitants. Just prior to Christmas 1659, Mary Longdon, a servant to gentleman and future mayor, John Pyne, refused to give Newton some of her master's beef. Newton had known Longdon for four years and was extremely angry at this refusal and left the scene grumbling. A week later, the women met once more, and Newton spilled a bucket of water Longdon carried on her head before violently kissing her and uttering a veiled threat. In the days that followed, Longdon reported being visited by the Devil and Newton in spirit form, and together they (unsuccessfully) tempted her to become a witch. Longdon then began to display symptoms that the local community readily recognised as demonic possession. She exhibited paranormal strength, experienced fits and trances, vomited household objects, and reacted badly to the touch of the Bible. Mysterious stones were also hurled at her master's house by unseen hands. Longdon also claimed to have been attacked by Newton in spectral form. The evidence against Newton mounted as she consecutively failed several traditional tests for witchcraft, including the ability to say the Lord's Prayer. She was further tested in prison while awaiting trial, before being accused of killing her jailor David Jones by kissing his hand through the bars of her cell. Florence Newton pleaded not guilty on 11 September 1661 at County Cork summer Assizes to two indictments: the bewitchment of Mary Longdon, which carried a maximum sentence of one year's imprisonment under the 1586 Irish Witchcraft Act, and the murder of David Jones, a capital crime for which the punishment was execution by hanging.[19] Historians have speculated that given the evidence against Newton, along with the fact that she was accused of a capital crime, it is probable she was convicted of witchcraft and executed shortly afterwards.[20] It has also been speculated that Newton may have died during the trial itself.[21]

Trial of Islandmagee Witches, County Antrim, 1711

The Islandmagee witches (eight women and one man) were tried and convicted in 1711 for the bewitchment of eighteen-year-old Mary Dunbar in two separate trials held in Carrickfergus at the spring and summer sessions of the County Antrim Assizes.[22] On 21 February 1711, in Islandmagee, an eight-mile-long peninsula on the east coast of County Antrim, which was home to 300 Presbyterians of Scots

---

'Gender, History and Witchcraft'; Lapoint, 'Irish Immunity', p. 82; Seymour, *Irish Witchcraft and Demonology*, chapter 5; Elmer, *Miraculous Conformist*, pp. 127–32.

[19] Sneddon, *Witchcraft and Magic in Ireland*, p. 27; 'An Act against Witchcraft and Sorcerie', 28 Eliz. I, c. 2 [Ireland] (1586).

[20] See Seymour, *Irish Witchcraft and Demonology*, pp. 107, 127; Lapoint, 'Irish Immunity', p. 75; Sneddon, *Witchcraft and Magic*, p. 78.

[21] Sneddon, 'Florence Newton's Trial', p. 304.

[22] The following narrative is based on: Sneddon, *Possessed by the Devil*; Sneddon, 'Witchcraft Belief, Representation and Memory', pp. 254–5.

descent, Mrs Ann Haltridge, the elderly widow of the local minister, Revd John Haltridge, died suddenly after months of supernatural attacks by a demon on her body and the home (Knowehead House) she shared with her servants, her son, his wife, and their young children. Five days after Ann was buried, her niece, Mary Dunbar, an educated, gentlewoman from Castlereagh, County Down, visited the mourning family in Knowehead House. Shortly after her arrival, Dunbar discovered the method of old Mrs Haltridge's bewitchment: image magic in the form of an apron bound tightly with string and containing the dead woman's missing flannel bonnet. Almost immediately, the demonic activity in the house reconvened, and a demon entered and possessed Dunbar, causing her to levitate; experience convulsions, fits, loss of speech, and appetite; and vomit household objects. In March 1711, Dunbar accused eight Presbyterian women of orchestrating her possession using witchcraft: Janet Liston (wife of William Sellor), Janet Carson, Catherine McCalmond, Margaret Mitchell, Janet Main, Janet Millar, Elizabeth Sellor (daughter of Janet Liston and William Sellor), and Janet Latimer. The Anglican-Whig Mayor of Carrickfergus, Edward Clements, then 'bound over' and jailed the accused women until their trial at the spring Assizes. Dunbar's symptoms continued up until the day of their trial and deprived her of speech and consequently the ability to give evidence in court. Despite pleading not guilty, on 31 March 1711, all eight women were convicted under the 1586 Irish Witchcraft Act for a first offence and were sentenced to one year's imprisonment and four appearances in the pillory on market day for six hours. Unlike most demoniacs, the incarceration of the accused did not lead to an improvement in Dunbar's health. Dunbar claimed this was because William Sellor had begun bewitching her. During the week that followed (early April 1711), Sellor was charged with bewitching Dunbar and on 11 September 1711 he was found guilty of witchcraft. Mary Dunbar died of unknown causes on 24 April 1711, three weeks after the first trial. Dunbar's death turned William's original crime of bewitchment into a capital offence for which the sentence was death by hanging. It is assumed that the sentence was carried out.

Mary Butters, County Antrim, 1807–1808

In the summer of 1807, in the small, Presbyterian, rural parish of Carnmoney, County Antrim, Alexander Montgomery, a tailor who lived close to the meeting house, began to panic when milk from his only cow could not be churned into butter.[23] Alexander's wife, Elizabeth concluded that the cow had been bewitched. Her suspicions were confirmed when she spoke to older women in the community who were able to recount similar tales. Elizabeth's female

---

[23] This account is based on: Sneddon, *Witchcraft and Magic in Ireland*, pp. 133–7. For more on Butters: Fulton, 'Clerics, Conjurors and Courtrooms', chapter 6.

Figure 1 John Boyne (c. 1750–1810), 'A Visit to a White Witch', 7 April 1800. Boyne was an engraver and watercolour painter born in County Down, Ireland, who worked in England and exhibited several works at the Royal Academy. Image courtesy of Karen Taylor Fine Art

network of knowledge was also a repository for amateur magical knowledge that could be used to deflect and fight unexplained forces that threatened life and limb. She was instructed by her network to tie branches of Rowan trees (also known as mountain ash and widely believed to have inherent magical properties) to the cow's tail and hang protective amulets in the cowshed. Elizabeth then gathered together twelve local women to bless the cow, which was then fed the ancient, herbal remedy and detoxifier and perennial flowering plant, vervain. When these actions failed, a professional cunning woman, Mary Butters, was called upon.[24] Irish people referred to cunning men and women (see Figure 1) in a variety of different ways. In English, they were known as wise men, wise women, fairy men, fairy women, fairy doctors, and elf doctors, while in Irish, they were called *doctúirí na síofraí* (fairy doctors), *bean chumhachtach* (woman with supernatural powers), *mná feasa* (wise women), and *bean feasa* (wise woman).[25] Confusingly, some of these terms were also used to describe charmers. Charmers differed from cunning folk in that they did not charge for their

---

[24] Hutton, *Witch*, p. xi.   [25] Jenkins, 'Biddy Early', p. 165.

services and specialised in curing naturally occurring illnesses or diseases in humans or animals; although some did provide charms to deflect or cure fairy or witch attacks.[26] '*Cailleach*', which translates from Irish as 'supernatural old woman' or 'hag', in Irish folk tradition could, depending on context, refer either to a cunning woman or healer or to witches who stole milk and butter.[27]

Mary Butters from nearby Carrickfergus was thirty-seven years old in 1807 and made a good living by curing bewitched cattle, telling fortunes, and finding stolen horses by divinatory methods. Butters arrived in Carnmoney on 18 August 1807 with a retinue of anti-witch measures at her disposal, which she employed consecutively to cure Montgomery's cow. She first churned its milk while repeating an incantation softly to herself, before drawing a circle around the churn and washing it in south-running water. When Elizabeth Montgomery found she was still unable to churn butter, Butters announced at nightfall she would try another charm that would not fail. She advised Alexander Montgomery and a local younger man, Carnaghan, to stand guard at the head of the bewitched cow with their waistcoats turned inside out. They were to remain there until Butters returned at midnight. Butters then went back to the Montgomery house with Elizabeth and her married, twenty-year-old son, David, and their elderly lodger, Margaret Lee. Butters then placed a large pot on the fire containing milk, sulphur, needles, large pins, and crooked nails. She then shut the door and sealed the chimney, windows, and doors with green turf. This counter spell was a type of sympathetic magic that worked in a similar way to seventeenth-century English witch bottles. The pan of milk was symbolic of the bladder of the witch deemed responsible for stealing Montgomery's butter, and the heat and sharp objects placed in it were designed to cause them intense pain. This pain would ultimately force them to reveal themselves while attempting to break the counter spell by overturning the milk pan. The openings in the house were sealed to prevent the witch from secretly entering the dwelling. Carnaghan and Alexander remained with the cow as Butters had instructed, but when she did not return as promised, the men left their post and returned to the house only to find Elizabeth and David dead. Montgomery's neighbours then brought Butters and Margaret Lee out of the house and into the fresh air. Butters made a full recovery, but Lee died shortly afterwards. An inquest was held into the deaths of Elizabeth, David, and Lee on 19 August 1807 by district coroner, James Stewart, before twelve jurors. It heard evidence from Alexander and his neighbour, William Greer, before ruling that all the deaths were the result of suffocation occasioned by the actions of Butters. In

---

[26] Sneddon, 'Magical Healing'; Wolf, 'Orthaí and Orthodoxy'; Moore, 'General Practice'.

[27] Ó Crualaoich, *Cailleach*; Lehane, 'Cailleach', pp. 189–90.

the hands of the legal system of the time, Butters' activities were viewed as unlawful killing, and she was arrested by local constables and placed in Carrickfergus jail to await trial for murder. On the day of her trial, in April 1808, the grand jury tasked with reviewing the evidence decided that it did not warrant grounds for a full trial before senior judges and a petty jury, and the case against her was discharged. According to local people interviewed in 1839, Mary Butters was still living in Carrickfergus and working as a cunning woman.[28] Local oral tradition suggested that she died in the town 'at an advanced age; some say she was 90'.[29] Alexander Montgomery did not spend long grieving for his wife and son. In November 1807, he married a sixteen-year-old woman, Miss Henderson, in Carnmoney. He was sixty years of age.[30]

2 Witchcraft and Magic in Modern Ireland

This section will suggest that belief in the supernatural, in particular witchcraft and harmful and beneficial magic, did not decline in Ireland between the eighteenth and late twentieth centuries. The legal position of magic certainly changed, and there were those who were sceptical of its existence, but belief continued, changing and developing in ways that often cut across established religious and political fault lines. It also continued to shape people's behaviour and the way they interacted with the world. Modern Ireland was therefore far from being disenchanted.

Witchcraft and Magic in Ireland, c. 1586–1922

In medieval and early modern Europe (c. 1420–1780), around 40,000-50,000 people were executed for witchcraft (of which 80 per cent were women), albeit in differing rates of intensity, at different times, for different reasons, and under different legal, political, and religious systems.[31] Ireland held only four trials under the 1586 Irish Witchcraft Act, some of which have already been mentioned: Marion Fisher, convicted (later pardoned) at County Antrim Assizes in Carrickfergus in 1655; Florence Newton, convicted in 1661; and the Islandmagee witches convicted in two trials held in 1711. These trials arose in late seventeenth-century Protestant (English and Scottish) settler communities, where belief in harmful, demonic witches formed part of a wider magical

---

[28] 'Fair Sheets by Thomas Fagan', Ordnance Survey Memoirs, Carnmoney, County Antrim, February–April 1839 (Public Record Office of Northern Ireland (PRONI), MIC 6C/Reel 2/ Box 6, Antrim VI, Carnmoney, p. 38).

[29] McGaw, 'Tragic Occurrence', p. 115.   [30] *Dublin Evening Post*, 26 November 1807.

[31] Any summary of early modern European witchcraft is an oversimplification, but the following works provide excellent surveys: Goodare, *European Witch-hunt*; Gibson, *Witchcraft: The Basics*; Levack, *Oxford Handbook of Witchcraft*.

culture where witchcraft accusation was not uncommon. However, prosecution and conviction rates remained low because of an increasingly sceptical, but not unbelieving, judiciary and clergy. The majority Catholic, largely Gaelic-speaking, Irish population, on the other hand, believed in witches but did not formally accuse or prosecute each other for witchcraft. This lack of witchcraft accusations in these communities is best explained by the low threat level that their culturally specific butter-stealing witches were believed to pose. Gaelic-Irish witches worked mostly at specific times of the traditional, ritual year, such as May Eve or May Day (1 May, or Bealtaine), were not considered demonic and did not usually harm or kill humans or livestock. Instead, they used magic to transfer the productiveness of their neighbours' milk to their own cows to increase their yield of butter. They were also believed to transmogrify into hares to steal milk directly from cows. Although the last Irish witchcraft trial occurred in 1711 and the 1586 Irish Witchcraft Act was repealed by the parliament of the United Kingdom in 1821, belief in witchcraft in Ireland did not decline during the long eighteenth century but changed and evolved as a result of cross-cultural fertilisation. The belief in butter-stealing witchcraft that had been so closely associated with Roman Catholic communities in the early modern period fused in eighteenth-century Protestant culture with existing notions of malefic, demonic witchcraft. Similarly, Gaelic-Irish witchcraft became more influenced by Protestant beliefs, resulting in a witch figure that was far more threatening to life, limb, and livestock.[32]

In the nineteenth and early twentieth centuries, witchcraft belief was strongest in rural areas, especially after the Great Famine of the 1840s, but can also be found in urban or proto-industrialised areas, especially in the north of Ireland. The homogenisation of witchcraft belief that occurred in the long eighteenth century should not be taken so far as to exclude the importance of regional and local differences. In Islandmagee, County Antrim, continuing belief in witchcraft was shaped by the social memory of the traumatic events of 1711, transmitted inter-generationally via a rich oral tradition and the folk heritage of places associated in popular culture with the trial. In the long nineteenth century, most witchcraft accusations were levied in small rural farming communities by disputing neigh-bours. They arose out of everyday squabbles, interactions, tensions, and soured relationships, rather than the sectarian and political divisions that had deepened with the rise of revolutionary nationalism in the 1860s and the civil unrest of the Land Wars that unfolded in the following decades. This social and interpersonal

---

[32] Sneddon, *Witchcraft and Magic in Ireland*, chapters 4–6. See also, Hutton, 'Witch-hunting in Celtic Societies', pp. 43–71. In more recent work, Hutton has been less willing to make a connection between belief in butter-stealing witchcraft and low prosecution rates: Hutton, *Witch*, pp. 248–50.

conflict was intensified in the post-famine period as economic, social, and gender relationships were challenged and realigned in a period of rapid and deep change. Nineteenth- and early twentieth-century Ireland remained predominantly Catholic, rural (although it was urbanising), and economically dependent on agriculture. Its population levels however plummeted during and after the Great Famine of the late 1840s, from death, hunger, disease, and emigration. In the sparsely populated countryside, women were increasingly ejected from public roles and paid employment in the context of increasingly restrictive patriarchy. As numbers of male agricultural labourers declined, those of small and larger tenant farmers grew: the latter benefitted from the consolidation of holdings and rising prices, while the former often found themselves in straitened economic circumstances, especially in times of downturn or rising rents. Consequently, misfortune to livestock and/or agricultural produce often had severe financial implications for smallholders. Living as these men and women did in a world still viewed very much in magical terms, any indication that witchcraft was involved was taken very seriously. Smallholders were thus the most likely to make witchcraft accusations against neighbours of similar economic means. Suspected witches on the other hand were male and female, formed part of the social and economic life of their communities, and often possessed a reputation for witchcraft. Just as in the early modern period, reputations were shaped and reshaped by gossip in rural communities by people they knew. In nineteenth-century Ireland, witchcraft accusers often took matters into their own hands by verbally abusing or physically assaulting suspected witches. These assaults were occasionally undertaken, as in England, as counter-magical measures. In most cases, however, they were acts of retaliatory violence conceived as ends in themselves. Thus, in common with most violent acts in nineteenth-century Ireland, they were personal in nature, directed against neighbours and friends during disputes. Witchcraft victims and other accusers also brought proceedings against suspected witches for statutory crimes such as theft, breach of the peace, and trespass. To magically counter bewitchment, they also employed cunning folk who occasionally found themselves in court when their unwitching services did not meet their client's expectations. As in the early modern period, suspected witches often did not accept accusations passively. They sought to protect or restore their honour and status by prosecuting accusers for slander or assault or by verbally or physically assaulting them. Legal recourse in these cases, whether sought by the accuser or the accused, was made easier from the 1830s onwards by the expansion of the summary court system and metropolitan and provincial policing.[33]

---

[33] Sneddon, 'Witchcraft Belief, Representation and Memory'; Sneddon and Fulton, 'Witchcraft'.

Although eighteenth-century reforming Catholic clerical elites condemned many popular folk beliefs they considered superstitious, malefic, demonic witch-craft retained its orthodoxy alongside other Church-sanctioned manifestations of the miraculous. Presbyterian Church Sessions and Presbyteries in Ulster, who were responsible for the moral conduct and behaviour of their congregations, mediated witchcraft accusations up until the early 1730s, after which time they were no longer taken seriously. Popular magic was another matter. Up until at least the 1790s, amateur dabblers in divination, cunning folk, and charmers were reprimanded by Presbyterian minsters and elders for un-Christian beliefs and practices. The moderate scepticism shown towards belief in witchcraft in the early eighteenth century by Church of Ireland clergy became more pronounced a few decades later, when it became increasingly acceptable to condemn it publicly in pamphlets, periodicals, and newspapers. Using classic enlightenment rhetoric, Protestants of the Anglican Ascendancy, who for much of the eighteenth-century monopolised power and property in Ireland, argued that witch trials were the product of religious zeal, intolerance, popular ignorance and superstition. Witchcraft thus belonged to an irrational age that Ascendancy Ireland, which they idealised as religiously moderate, stable, rational, and constantly improving, had moved beyond. The fact that a large majority of the population still believed in witchcraft and 'beneficial' magic was ignored, and when contemporary witchcraft was discussed in print in eighteenth-century Ireland, it was othered as a problem of indigenous populations of British colonies such as Jamaica, or of benighted Roman Catholic countries such as Poland or Spain.[34]

Although the nineteenth century was a period of religious reform and revival in Ireland, the majority Churches (Anglican, Presbyterian, and Roman Catholic), along with smaller denominations such as Methodism, remained largely silent on the issue of continued popular belief in witchcraft. The eighteenth-century minor-ity Anglican position, that belief in witchcraft was 'superstitious' and the product of an age of unreason righted only by enlightened rationalism, became the accepted mainstream, public position in the nineteenth century, for Catholics and Protestants, Unionists and Nationalists. It is particularly noticeable in the sentencing and summing-up of magistrates presiding over cases involving witch-craft, and in newspaper editorials, opinion pieces, and court reporting.[35] However, public professions of disbelief could have masked very different (or

---

[34] Sneddon, *Witchcraft and Magic in Ireland*, pp. 66–70, 99–100, 104–16; Minutes of the Presbytery of Moira and Lisburn, 26 December 1781, Hillhall, County Down (PRONI, Stewart Ms, D1759/1/D/22); Roseyard Presbyterian Church Session Book, 17 October 1795 (PRONI, Tennant Papers, D1748/A/2/31, p. 105).

[35] Sneddon, 'Witchcraft, Representation and Memory', p. 261; Sneddon and Fulton, 'Witchcraft', pp. 6–9. See also section 3.

at the very least ambivalent) private views that individuals were unable or unwilling to share openly. This may have been for reasons of political or social expediency, or for fear of damaging reputations by conflicting with public expectations of taste and fashion.[36] Unfortunately, as Malcolm Gaskill has pointed out, 'we cannot write a history of private conscience; a history of public performance, however, is more readily within our grasp'.[37] This tension between private conscience and public performance was certainly present in nineteenth-century, middle-class, rural County Antrim, where many of the educated middle class still believed in fairies, witchcraft, and charms but were careful not to share their views about them until they trusted the person they were talking to.[38]

Witchcraft and Magic in Ireland, c.1921–1998

Thus, in eighteenth- and nineteenth-century Ireland, profound scepticism of magic and witchcraft may have affected only a small part of a disproportionately loud and politically influential, male Irish population: we know little of what elite women thought about witchcraft in this period, privately or publicly. However, for many ordinary Irish men and women, witchcraft, and the ability to counter it using magical means, remained either a reality or at the very least, a possibility. What happened to witchcraft and popular after partition in 1921 remains largely unclear, as this is the date at which recent, dedicated studies ended.[39] There is however increasing evidence that a vibrant magical culture existed in twentieth-century Ireland. Cara Delay has uncovered the gendered nature of stories and legends of fairies, charmers, and wise women (cunning folk) that permeated Ireland's rural, oral life between the late nineteenth and mid twentieth century. She has argued that magical culture in rural Catholic Ireland, especially for women, was used to contest and negotiate a modernising Church and state, and to thwart and resist British

---

[36] For this negotiation between public performance and/or duty and private belief in seventeenth- and eighteenth-century England, see: Barry, 'Public Infidelity and Private Belief', pp. 117–43; Gaskill, *Crime and Mentalities*, pp. 118–19.

[37] Gaskill, *Crime and Mentalities*, p. 119.

[38] *Belfast Morning News*, 2 June 1859; *Belfast Newsletter* (*BNL*), 11 August 1888; Day and McWilliams, *Ordnance Survey Memoirs*, pp. x, 40–1. The OSMI were parish accounts for the North of Ireland compiled by several collectors in the 1830s and early 1840s to accompany the new 6-inch ordnance survey maps. They were published in Belfast in the 1990s. The OSMI, along with the Ordnance Survey letters (OSL) written by collectors, provide indispensable 'ethnographic fieldwork on topography and local history' and a guide to the 'Irish vernacular landscape', where folklore, folk history and folk commemoration are embedded in the landscape: Beiner, *Year of the French*, p. 15. The OSL, which are only partly published, are an important source of folklore which provide insight into supernatural belief systems and traditions: McDonough, 'Folk Belief and Landscape', pp. 56–69.

[39] Fulton, 'Clerics, Conjurors and Courtrooms'; Sneddon and Fulton, 'Witchcraft'; Sneddon, *Witchcraft and Magic in Ireland*.

colonial power.[40] Thomas Waters has argued that belief in supernatural cursing (inherently different to witchcraft as it only targeted perceived wrongdoers) was widespread in Ireland until at least the mid-twentieth century, 'when its major uses disappeared and the networks that transmitted knowledge about it atrophied'.[41] In a now classic study, Patricia Lysaght demonstrated that firm belief in the supernatural death messenger, the Banshee or Bean Sí, was reflected in Irish folklore up until the late twentieth century.[42]

Sociologist Richard Jenkins has scrutinised rumours and fears surrounding black magic and modern Satanism in conflict-torn Northern Ireland in the early 1970s within the context of wider, continued belief in the supernatural: from fairies, ghosts, divination, and magical healing to death messengers. He also detailed the activities of a group of British Army Intelligence Officers, operating out of Lisburn, County Antrim, between 1973 and 1974, who fabricated 'black magic sites' in Northern Ireland to (literally) demonise paramilitary organisations, and to frighten local children into staying off the streets at night and away from Army observation posts.[43] Islandmagee was selected as one of these sites because of its long-standing association with witchcraft, in particular the Islandmagee witch trial of 1711.[44] The rationale being that Islandmagee's association with early modern Satanic witches made it easier for people to believe that an organised sect of devil-worshipers were practising black magic in the present day. This was not the first time that witchcraft and Satanism were mentioned in conjunction with one another in relation to Islandmagee. In October 1961, the Irish daily newspaper, the *Irish Press*, reported that Northern Ireland's police force, the Royal Ulster Constabulary (RUC), were investigating a 'black magic' cult in Islandmagee after cyclists found objects in a cave believed to have been used in a Satanic ritual, including black candles and black cloaks. An RUC spokesman at the time stated that although the 'witches coven' responsible had abandoned the cave, they could return at any time. He further remarked, erroneously, that, 'a 14th century Witchcraft Act prohibits such activities'.[45] This appropriation of the image of the early modern witch to fuel a Satanic scare occurred on a far larger scale in Britain and North America in the 1980s. Ronald Hutton has argued this panic over ritual Satanic child abuse was 'based firmly on the early modern construct of an international, devil-worshipping sect concealed within Western societies'

---

[40] Delay, *Irish Women*, pp. 176–81, 216–18.

[41] Waters, 'Irish Cursing', pp. 113–49 (quote at p. 142). See also, Waters, *Cursed Britain*, pp. 42–8.

[42] Lysaght, *Banshee*, especially pp. 15–26, 219–43; *Blúiríní Béaloidis*, 27.

[43] Jenkins, *Black Magic and Bogeymen*. See also, Jenkins, 'Spooks and Spooks'.

[44] Jenkins, *Black Magic and Bogeymen*, pp. 53, 83–5, 87.

[45] *Irish Press*, 4 October 1961; Sneddon, 'Witchcraft, Representation and Memory', p. 259. See also, *Belfast Telegraph* (*BT*), 3 October 1961.

but 'repackaged in a form suitable for rationalists', so all that was required was the belief that a group of well-organised, practicing Satanists were committing criminal and antisocial acts and thus had to be rooted-out and punished.[46] Satanism grew in the second half of the twentieth century and variously comprised Satanic abuse mythologies, the threat devil-worship was believed to pose to Christianity, and veritable, practiced Satanism most notable in the formation of Satanist churches, beginning with the Church of Satan in San Francisco in 1966.[47] Jenny Butler's ethnographic study of Pagan witchcraft (including Wicca) in the Republic of Ireland in the twenty-first century has revealed it to be a vibrant and pervasive religious culture that is able and content to draw on Ireland's linguistic and cultural heritage, including its history, mythology, and folklore.[48] While folkloric and ethnographic studies conducted across the island of Ireland in the late twentieth century have uncovered widespread belief in, and use of, faith and magical healing.[49]

Despite our increasing knowledge of modern Irish magical mentalities, self-identifying witches, and the links made between Satanism and witchcraft, we know little of what happened to the type of the witches feared in Ireland before 1922, or indeed of the cunning folk who countered them. An initial survey of Irish newspapers, folklore and material culture indicates that the demise in belief in witchcraft in Britain in the first half of the twentieth century did not occur in Ireland, where it retained some cultural currency in rural areas up until the twenty-first century. This difference is perhaps not surprising given that some of the key factors identified as causing the British decline in the early part of the twentieth century are not applicable to Ireland, namely the rise of scientific medicine and a decline in oral storytelling, popular Christianity, and the provision of unwitching services. Throughout the twentieth century, Irish magical specialists treated conditions thought to have been inflicted supernaturally (see later in the text), and any decline in oral tradition, due to competition from cinema, television, radio and print material, occurred towards the end of the century.[50] Crawford Gribben has argued that the secularisation of Irish society did not begin until the 1990s, and it was far more rapid and keenly felt in the Republic than in Northern Ireland. This period witnessed a decline in church attendance and numbers of clergy trained, along with a diminishment of the role of churches in social teaching and in shaping public policy.[51]

---

[46] Hutton, *Witch*, p. 42.

[47] La Fontaine, 'Satanism and Satanic Mythology', pp. 83–140; Fexneld, 'Disciples of Hell', pp. 334, 339–44.

[48] Butler, 'Nearest Kin of the Moon'. For a classic study of pagan witchcraft in the British Isles: Hutton, *Triumph of the Moon*.

[49] Moore, 'General Practice'; Buckley, 'Unofficial Healing'; Doherty, 'Cattle Diseases'.

[50] Lysaght, *Banshee*, pp. 235–7.   [51] Gribben, *Rise and Fall*, pp. 199–209.

Furthermore, in Ireland (and in diaspora communities abroad), from its rise in the late eighteenth century to its consolidation in the nineteenth and twentieth centuries, scientific, professional medicine, institutionalised in the public health system, was often used instead of, or in conjunction with, traditional folk medicine and magical healing. Scientific medicine was thus able to coincide with magical belief without necessarily replacing or diminishing it.[52] Although professional health care is widely available and accessible across the island of Ireland in the twenty-first century, charms and charming are still widely used.[53]

A survey of Irish digitised newspapers published between 1922 and 1998[54] uncovered only two criminal cases involving witchcraft, one from Northern Ireland and one from the Irish Free State. In 1927, Isabella Hazelton, an apparently respectable and 'well dressed woman' of Drumcrow, County Tyrone, charged neighbours, William Blair, and Issac and Sarah McFarland, of Drumhorrick, County Tyrone with slander. The resulting court case held at Strabane Quarter Sessions, County Tyrone established that the slander was rooted in local gossip spread by the defendants that Isabella had used the evil eye (blinking) to transfer the productiveness from her neighbour's milk to her own to create a bountiful supply of butter. At the trial, Halzelton claimed that although she did not believe in 'blinking' the whole district in which she lived did, and as a result even children refused to speak to her.[55] Presiding Judge Linehan ruled that although blinking 'was outlandish and highly improbable' it was nevertheless slanderous to accuse some one of it because so many local people believed in its power.[56] The Judge dismissed the evidence against Sarah and Issac MacFarland and the other defendants on a technicality but ruled that the 'gross scandal of Blair' had been proven by several witnesses. He awarded damages to Isabella amounting to £5, to be paid by Blair.[57] The evil eye was an innate, harmful, magical power located in the eyes that could be used both intentionally and unintentionally. Among early modern Protestant settlers in Ireland, 'overlooking' referred specifically to the unintentional evil eye, while witchcraft described its intentional use. The intentional evil eye was first linked to the activities of butter and milk-stealing witches in Gaelic-Irish

---

[52] Cox, 'Access and Engagement', pp. 57–78; Cox, 'Medical Marketplace', pp. 55–79; Foley, 'Indigenous Narratives', pp. 5–18; Linn, 'Irish Immigrant Healing Magic', pp. 144–65; Davies, *America Bewitched*, pp. 104–5; Moore, 'General Practice', pp. 104–29.

[53] Wolf, 'Orthaí and Orthodoxy', p. 128; *Irish Times* (*IT*), 26 October 2013.

[54] This search was conducted in 2020, using digitised newspapers published in Ireland and accessed via: Irish Newspaper Archives, www.irishnewsarchive.com; British Library/ Findmypast Newspaper Archive Limited, The British Newspaper Archive, www .britishnewspaperarchive.co.uk/.

[55] Crown Files at Quarter Sessions, Division of Dungannon, 1927 (PRONI, TYR/1/B/2/36); *Anglo-Celt*, 15 October 1927; *Irish Independent* (*II*), 27 October 1927; *Northern Whig*, 28 October 1927.

[56] *Anglo-Celt*, 15 October 1927.   [57] *II*, 27 October 1927.

culture in the later medieval period. The term 'blinking' emerged in the modern period to describe both witches who used the evil eye to steal butter and milk and those who used it to harm or kill cattle and humans. It was occasionally used to describe the unintentional use of the evil eye.[58]

In January 1933, the *Southern Star* reported that the District Justice presiding over Ballyjamesduff District Court, County Cavan, had refused an application made by an ex-sergeant of the Royal Irish Constabulary, Peter Scully, to have his neighbour, John Lynch, a farmer, 'bound to [keep] the peace'. The action was a result of crossed wires over the meaning of a local magical custom. It began when Scully asked Lynch to have a 'brash' at churning the butter that his servant was making in his kitchen. Scully stated in court, through his solicitor, that requests of this type were customary in his local area and were used 'to prevent the fairies bringing the butter away'. Lynch refused to comply with Scully's request because he believed it could put him under suspicion of witchcraft, or as he put it, accused of trying to steal the 'butter off the churn'. A scuffle ensued and Lynch was accused of shouting at Scully, 'You will put me under no process for witchery'. The judge deemed the whole case 'absurd', while a court reporter referred to it in his byline as a 'Cavan Court Comedy'.[59]

The cessation of court cases involving witchcraft in the early 1930s could, of course, be taken as an indication of a demise in belief. Some educated, sceptical urban dwellers were certainly convinced that this was the case. In December 1945, from his manse in Athlone, a town that lay on the border of counties Roscommon and Westmeath, Revd Hugh J. Ritchie wrote in a letter to the editor of the *Westmeath Examiner* that 'it is not impossible that the belief in strong drink and the supportive qualities of alcohol will become as obsolete as the belief in witchcraft'.[60] Reporters on the other hand who had spent time talking with people in rural Northern Ireland saw things differently. A column titled, 'Around and About', published in the *Belfast Newsletter* in 1935, stated that 'in parts of County Tyrone they do really believe, apparently in the blinking of cattle, and many farmers have a genuine belief that there are people who possess the power to cast an evil spell over animals, so that they die or go into ill

---

[58] Glanvill, *Saducismus Triumphatus*, p. 379; Hutton, 'Witch-hunting in Celtic Societies', pp. 59, 64–5; Larner, *Enemies of God*, p. 8; Ady, *Candle in the Dark*, p. 104; William Molyneux's Commonplace book, 1683 (Trinity College, Dublin (TCD) Molyneux Papers, Ms 883/1, p. 297); Scot, *Discoverie of Witchcraft*, pp. 36–7; Borsje, *Celtic Evil Eye*, pp. 16–17, 48–54, 76–7; F.M.A., 'Witch-stones', Ballymena, County Antrim, 1963 (Ulster Folk and Transport Museum (UFTM), Questionnaires, 63/Q2b/0095).

[59] *Southern Star*, 7 January 1933. For Scully's RIC service record: Constabulary Force Funds, 1 November 1941 (National Archives, Kew, Royal Irish Constabulary Service Records, HO 184/221).

[60] *Westmeath Examiner*, 29 December 1945.

health'.[61] Ireland's unusually rich collection of folklore also suggests that witchcraft remained of some concern to rural people, and that they continued to suspect neighbours of practising it. The decline in court cases may indicate that people were less likely to openly trade harsh words or fists because of these suspicions, and instead turned quietly to apotropaic magic or the occasional intervention of unwitchers. As the twentieth century wore on, it may have become harder to convince magistrates or members of an increasingly professionalised police service to take criminal matters involving witchcraft or magic seriously.

Irish folklore encompasses beliefs customs and material culture and is dynamic and evolving. It has increasingly been used as a historical source because it throws light upon aspects of the lives and mental worlds of the poor (especially women) that would have otherwise went undocumented, including supernatural beliefs and practices.[62] Historians of Ireland have moved beyond regarding folklore primarily as a way 'to find additional information to augment a historical account that is largely framed by more conventional print and manuscript sources'.[63] It is now viewed more as a source in its own right that enables the study of Irish mentalities and those parts of popular culture that lie outside of professional historiographies.[64] Folklore is thus positioned as vernacular discourse that allows access to community memories, narratives and traditions.[65] Published folklore in the nineteenth and early twentieth centuries was collected from tenant farmers and smallholders by (mainly) Protestant, Anglo-Irish, landowning elites, and dealt primarily with what was pejoratively termed 'superstitious' supernatural practices and beliefs, including witchcraft, fairies, divination, and magical healing. In 1935, the Irish Folklore Commission (IFC) was established in the Irish Free State as part of its 'Gaelicisation' policy, along with the revival of the Irish language. It aimed to gather folklore (especially in rural, Irish-speaking areas) to document and retrieve the unwritten beliefs, customs, and narratives of the Irish people. By emphasising tradition and cultural continuities between the ancient, Celtic past and contemporary Ireland, the IFC aimed to bolster Irish nationalism and nationalist heritage, legitimise the new Irish state, and heal the deep divisions resulting from the war of independence and the civil war.[66] The records of the IFC were archived in 1971 in the Department of Folklore, University College,

---

[61] *BNL*, 27 March 1935. This article was republished by the *Mid-Ulster Mail*, 6 April 1935.

[62] Breathnach, 'Handywomen and Birthing', pp. 34–6, 45–7; Tait, 'Worry Work', p. 218; McDonough, 'Folk Belief and Landscape', pp. 56–69.

[63] Daly, 'State Papers', pp. 70–6 (quote at p. 77).

[64] Beiner, *Year of the French*, pp. 12–13, 15.

[65] Beiner, *Year of the French*, p. 30; Daly, 'State Papers', p. 78.

[66] Daly, 'State Papers', pp. 66–7; Ó Giolláin, *Locating Irish Folklore*, p. 129.

Dublin. This archive was renamed the National Folklore Collection (NFC) in 2005, of which the manuscripts from the Schools Folklore Scheme (SFS) form an important part. Between 1937 and 1938, the SFS encouraged children in 5,000 primary schools to collect folklore from their communities under the guidance of their teachers. The Committee on Ulster Folklife and Traditions was established in Northern Ireland in 1953, and two years later it founded the *Ulster Folklife* journal. Influenced by the IFC, the committee began collecting folklore via voluntary subscribers who filled-out field notebooks and completed questionaries. In the early 1960s, the Committee created the Ulster Folklife Society (UFS), which continued to collect folklore and took over the publication of *Ulster Folklife*. This material is currently housed in the Ulster Folk and Transport Museum (UFTM) near Belfast. The UFTM was created when the Ulster Folk Museum in Cultra Manor (established in 1958 by the Northern Irish parliament) merged with the Belfast Transport Museum in 1967.[67]

Irish folklore, from folk narratives and belief statements to customs and legends, paints a vivid picture of witchcraft and magic in Ireland in twentieth-century Ireland. It suggests that belief in, and fear of witchcraft receded deeper into the countryside as the century progressed, where oral tradition remained especially strong, and where the loss of livestock, by magical means or otherwise, was more keenly felt and thus more feared. In 1922, Limerick-born antiquarian, Thomas Johnson Westropp, the son of a substantial landowner, in a study of folklore from Connacht in the west of Ireland, noted that '"the Dead Hand" was used there for "taking" milk and butter: i.e. forcing the cattle of the owner to give more milk taken from those of his neighbours'.[68] The right hand was first removed from a corpse, dried, smoked and 'subjected to certain spells'.[69] W.B. Yeats in his folklore anthology, *Fairy and Folk Tales of the Irish Peasantry* (1888),[70] wrote that of the 'spells of the witch' one of the 'most powerful is the charm of the dead hand'. In Yeats' version, the sympathetic magic at the heart of the spell relied on the skimming water from a neighbour's land: 'With a hand cut from a corpse, they, muttering words of power, will stir a well and skim from its surface a neighbour's butter'.[71] The use of corpses in

---

[67] For overviews of the history of folklore collection in nineteenth- and twentieth-century Ireland: Ó Giolláin, *Locating Irish Folklore*, chapters 2, 4; Breathnach, 'Handywomen and Birthing', pp. 34–9, 43–5; Briody, *Irish Folklore Commission*.

[68] Westropp, 'Folklore on the Coasts of Connacht', p. 390.

[69] Westropp, 'Folklore on the Coasts of Connacht', p. 390. For Westropp: Irwin, 'Westropp'.

[70] The literature on Yeats is copious and includes: Foster, *W. B. Yeats: A Life, I, 1865–1914*; Foster, *W. B. Yeats: A Life, II, 1915–1939*; Harper, *Yeats and the Occult*; Brown, *Life of W. B. Yeats*.

[71] Yeats, *Fairy and Folk Tales*, p. 148.

magic and medicine is well documented, and can be found in Roman antiquity, in early modern Europe, and in Victorian England.[72]

In common with Cailleach, the Irish language term, pishogues (or piseogs) had various meanings and depending on context could refer to 'a superstitious belief or practice, or ... a charm or [evil] spell'.[73] In this latter 'context the enactment of piseogs were essentially a form of folk witchcraft, a form of malevolent magic to wish misfortune or even death on someone'.[74] Some even claimed, in the early twentieth century, that 'Pishoge [*sic*] is the Irish for witchcraft'.[75] For the most part, however, it was used to describe a specific form of harmful transference and sympathetic magic: eggs or sheaves of corn were buried on the land of target individuals and families, usually by neighbours, and as they rotted their 'luck' or health (or that of their livestock) declined or waned. Diseased animal carcasses were also buried in the hope that the disease would be magically (not biologically) transferred onto landowner's cattle.[76] On at least one occasion this led to a court case. In County Clare, in October 1943, Mrs Mary Burke was brought before Ennis District Court for using threatening language against neighbours Martin and Thomas Lynch. The Lynch family informed the court that Burke had told them that she had lit fires on their land to transfer onto their livestock the pishogues she believed they had used to kill her cattle. District Justice D.F. Gleeson remarked that irrespective of their efficacy, her actions were taken very seriously in that part of the world, so warranted his bounding her over to keep the peace for twelve months.[77] Pishogues were also linked to butter-stealing witchcraft. In the mid-1930s, in counties Limerick, Mayo, Tyrone, Cork, and Waterford, the term was used by both English and Irish speakers to describe witches who employed charms to steal milk and butter from their neighbours' cows.[78]

Witches who used the evil eye rather than charms or pishogues were particularly feared in inter- and pre-war Ulster. In County Armagh, in the late 1920s, a local farmer told folklorist T.G.F Paterson, 'that the kind [of people] that wur

---

[72] Davies and Matteoni, *Executing Magic*, p. 1.

[73] McGarry, 'Guide to Piseogs'. For an early discussion of the multiple meanings of pishogues: 'Poll the Pishogue', *Northern Whig*, 13 January 1842.

[74] McGarry, *Irish Customs and Rituals*, p. 150.   [75] *Nenagh Guardian*, 30 January 1926.

[76] 'A Remarkable Case', *Cork Examiner*, 21 December 1909; National Folklore Collection (NFC), Schools Collection, Vol. 0513, p. 523; Vol. 0979, p. 216; McGarry, 'Guide to Piseogs'; Waters, *Cursed Britain*, p. 46.

[77] *Limerick Leader*, 4 October 1943.

[78] NFC, Schools Collection, Vol. 0311, p. 34; Vol. 0520, p. 31; Vol. 0656, p. 109; Vol. 0133, p. 460. The word 'Pishogues' was used in Tipperary in 1895 to describe the activities of a suspected witch assaulted by a neighbour for magically stealing milk from his cows: 'The Belief in Pishogues', *Newry Reporter*, 8 October 1895. For a similar case that occurred a few years earlier in the village of Finuge, County Kerry: *Kerry Sentinel*, 14 May 1892.

born blinkers were tarrable', if 'ye had cows that wur milkin' well, they'd coax the milk till theirselves. Or if it wus the butter they wanted, they'd wait till ye churned an' then ye'd have none! It was the same with crops too'.[79] In the late 1930s, in Clooney, County Donegal, in the Irish Free State, Mrs McBride told a collector for the IFC that, 'May Eve . . . was a great day for blinking and some people used to take away milk from other people's cows'.[80] In May 1942, Sam Henry, folklorist, broadcaster, and civil servant (born in Coleraine in County Londonderry) wrote to Dr John Davy Rolleston, a physician with an interest in the history and folklore of medicine, to tell him about local 'superstitions'. Henry informed Rolleston that he knew people in Northern Ireland, in both English and Gaelic-speaking districts, who still feared the evil eye and the threat it posed to their cows and agricultural produce.[81] In fieldnotes, typed-up during a trip to Rathlin Island in 1937, a mostly Roman Catholic, rural community on the north coast of Northern Ireland, Henry noted bluntly that, 'the island [was] ruined with witchcraft'.[82]

Henry's suspicions were confirmed in the summers of 1953 and 1954, when Michael Murphy visited Rathlin to collect folklore on behalf of the IFC.[83] Murphy was the sole full-time collector for the IFC (appointed in the late 1940s) who worked in Northern Ireland, and one of only two who did so exclusively in the English language.[84] During his trips, Murphy was informed of local men and women who were suspected of transforming into witch-hares to steal milk; of women who skimmed dew from their neighbour's land to transfer the profit from their neighbour's milk to their own to increase butter yield, and of charmers who possessed charms to heal humans who had been 'blinked'.[85] In the twentieth century, witch-hares feature most prominently in an migratory Irish legend that is also found in Britain, Germany and North America: a witch-hare is shot by a farmer or hunter while stealing milk from a cow, and when it is followed it leads the shooter to a house or cabin where an old woman is found bleeding from the exactly the same place on her body where

---

[79] Paterson, *County Cracks*, pp. 42–3.   [80] NFC, Schools Collection, Vol. 1087, p. 232.
[81] Sam Henry, 'Letter Referring to Superstitions', 28 May 1942 (Coleraine Museum, Sam Henry Collection, p. 1). For Rolleston: Underwood, 'Dr. J. D. Rolleston', p. 506.
[82] Sam Henry, 'Rathlin Island', 6 August 1937 (Coleraine Museum, Sam Henry Collection).
[83] Murphy, *Rathlin*, pp. vi, vii.   [84] Briody, *Irish Folklore Commission*, p. 457.
[85] Murphy, *Rathlin*, pp. 50–2. For more place and person specific, twentieth-century folklore concerning butter stealing-witches and witch-hares: Ó Muirithe and Nuttall, *Folklore of County Wexford*, pp. 75, 77–8, 95; Cashman, 'Neighborliness and Decency, Witchcraft and Famine', pp. 79–100; Glassie, *Ballymenone*, p. 536. Late nineteenth- and twentieth-century folklore, from counties as far apart Leitrim on the west coast and Wexford on the east, abounds with narratives of witches who skimmed dew from their neighbours' grass, for example: Duncan, 'Notes from Co. Leitrim', pp. 184–5; NFC, Schools Collection, Vol. 0885, p. 256; Vol. 0886, pp. 99–100.

the hare was wounded. In this way, her witchcraft is revealed to the world.[86] Some migratory legends however did not reflect real-world belief in, or fear of, witches. The legend of the ship-sinking witch has been documented in folklore from all over north-western Europe, especially in coastal regions, and in nineteenth- and early twentieth-century Ireland, from Donegal, to Sligo and Mayo. In a prominent redaction, an old widow, skilled in the black arts and possessing a long reputation for witchcraft, uses sympathetic magic to raise a storm at sea to drown fishermen who have refused her charity or wronged her in some way.[87] There is no evidence however that Irish people formally or informally accused each other of magically sinking ships in either the early modern or modern eras.

Around the same time Murphy was working on Rathlin, folklorist Jeanne Cooper Foster found that in other parts of Ulster witches were believed to blink pigs as well as humans and cows. A Presbyterian clergyman from Tyrone even informed her that a woman from his congregation, who believed she had been blinked, had been cured by a local cunning man.[88] In the late 1970s and early 1980s, ethnographer Henry Glassie, while studying the rural community of Ballymenone, County Fermanagh, in Northern Ireland, met a range of people who sincerely believed that witches had stolen milk and butter using charms, the evil eye, and by skimming dew from their neighbours' grass.[89] In 2000, folklorist Michael Doherty sent 'a questionnaire ... to all registered members of the veterinary profession in the Republic of Ireland' and 'to selected veterinarians in the six counties of Northern Ireland'.[90] Doherty received replies from seventy-three veterinarians, and at least one from each of the thirty-two counties.[91] They reported that red flannel was still employed (albeit rarely) to protect cattle and humans from evil forces in County Tyrone,[92] and that in counties Donegal, Tyrone and Limerick some farmers believed that animals (including horses) could be 'blinked' by witches.[93]

In twentieth-century Ireland, people still believed in, and at some level, feared harmful magic but how widespread or deeply held this was is impossible to quantify. As Patricia Lysaght pointed out in her study of the Banshee, there are inherent difficulties in gauging the level of supernatural belief at any given time. Some people believed all their lives, while others remained confirmed sceptics. Then, as has been mentioned, there were those who privately believed but were frightened, for a variety of reasons, of publicly admitting credulity.

---

[86] Nildin-Wall and Wall, 'Witch as Hare', pp. 67, 71–2.
[87] Mac Cárthaigh, 'Ship-Sinking Witch'.   [88] Foster, *Ulster Folklore*, pp. 86–9.
[89] Glassie, *Ballymenone*, pp. 534–9.   [90] Doherty, 'Cattle Diseases', pp. 41–75 (p. 41).
[91] Doherty, 'Cattle Diseases', p. 42.   [92] Doherty, 'Cattle Diseases', p. 69.
[93] Doherty, 'Cattle Diseases', p. 55.

People's views also changed over the course of their lives: they could begin as sceptics but end their lives as convinced believers, and vice versa, due to lifestyle changes, specific events, or wider religious or social influences.[94] What is clear is that whatever their public position on the supernatural was, many Irish people in the twentieth century believed enough in witchcraft or fairies to alter their behaviour in some way. Up until the twenty-first century, farmers, and road planners, especially in the south of Ireland, avoided the misfortune believed to accompany the destruction of fairy thorns (usually Hawthorn or Rowan trees) by circumnavigating them when ploughing fields or building motorways.[95] Since starting Ulster University in 2008, I routinely asked students whether they believed in fairies, to which around 90–95 per cent answered in the negative. However, only around 70 per cent said they would cut down a fairy tree, which is suggestive of either a reluctance to admit they believed in fairies in public, or of cognitive dissonance: where people believe they do not believe in fairies but are nevertheless frightened at some level of the consequences of upsetting them. Furthermore, deep into the twentieth century, Irish farmers continued to employ magical protection against witch and fairy attack. Folklore, ethnographic, and historical studies conducted all over the island, from counties Dublin, Mayo, and Cork, to Antrim, Leitrim, and Cavan, suggest that up until at least the 1970s those engaged in domestic butter production used a variety of apotropaic charms and rituals to protect the churn. We have already come across the practice of making visitors bless it, or to wish it good luck, but coins were also placed in a pail of the milk of a newly freshened cow to ensure it continued to milk. On or around May Day, the churn was protected by placing Rowan trees around it, and salt was placed on the lid or inside the churn itself. Iron objects, including tongs, nails, and pokers, were also placed into, underneath, and around it.[96]

In Ulster, witch-stones (also known as elf or fairy-stones) were naturally holed pebbles or stones usually (but not always) hung on string in byres or around the necks of cows to protect them from attack.[97] They were also used in early modern and modern Scotland and England as magical protective devices, where they were also known as 'mare' or 'hag' stones.[98] Objects relating to magical culture are increasingly used by archaeologists and historians to

---

[94] Lysaght, *Banshee*, pp. 219–22, 230–4.

[95] NFC, Schools Collection, Vol. 1028, p. 412, County Donegal; 'Fairy Thorn', County Armagh, May 1969, NFC, Photographic Collection, F037.25.00006; 'Fairy Bush [Co. Clare] Survives the Motorway Planners', *IT*, 29 May 1999.

[96] Lehane, 'Cailleach', pp. 190–1; Akenson, *Two Revolutions*, pp. 135–6.

[97] Dent, 'Witch-stone in Ulster and England', pp. 46–8; Sneddon, 'Witchcraft, Representation and Memory', p. 255.

[98] Davies and Houlbrook, *Building Magic*, pp. 108–11.

explore how magic was used, understood, and practised in both the early modern and modern periods.[99] The UFTM has a fine example of a witch-stone that was hung in a cowshed or byre in County Tyrone up until the 1930s.[100] While in 1937, a young, voluntary collector for the IFC, Charles McAfee, drew and described a 'protective pebble' or 'witch-stone' that he saw suspended in a byre in Ballycastle, County Antrim.[101] Benefitting from modern technology, in October 1958, IFC collector Michael Murphy photographed an 'elf-stone' in the coastal village of Cushendall, County Antrim.[102] A few years later, in 1962, a folklore collector for the UFS, noted that a variety of charms (including witch-stones) were used in the village to protect 'milk and butter' because 'your cow could be "blinked"'.[103] Two witch-stones also hung in a byre on a farm in Islandmagee until the 1970s, at which time they were deposited in the UFTM. Literary sources confirm that witch-stones were used in the peninsula at that time as a protection against witchcraft.[104]

Conclusion

In twentieth-century rural Ireland belief in witchcraft was either firmly held or lingered as a possibility to be called upon as an explanatory mechanism in certain circumstances. This was a population that worked (or had until recently) the land and kept or cared for livestock, and their witches largely stole milk and butter or harmed or killed animals using charms, incantations, and the wilful use of the evil eye. This prominence of the evil eye, especially in the north of Ireland, marked a change from the previous century, as did the decline in reportage of witch-hares, which nevertheless retained a strong presence in migratory legends. Furthermore, unlike in the nineteenth century, twentieth-century witches were not fought using words or physical violence (which explains the drop in slander and assault cases that involved an accusation of witchcraft) but by cunning folk and the use of apotropaic magic. Caveats aside, in relation to gauging levels of supernatural belief, it is also apparent that belief in, and fear of, witchcraft in Ireland was not as pervasive in the twentieth century as it had been in the nineteenth century. Although an extensive oral history and folklore project, covering north and

---

[99] See: Dowd, 'Bewitched', pp. 541–73; Merrifield, *Archaeology of Ritual and Magic*; Houlbrook and Armitage, *Materiality of Magic*; Hutton, *Physical Evidence*.

[100] Mr Laverty (donator), 'Witch-stone from Cookstown, Co. Tyrone', 1965 (UFTM, Object, 104.1965).

[101] NFC, Main Manuscript Collection, Vol. 0323, p. 8.

[102] NFC, Photographic Collection, I045.24.00001.

[103] Interview, Mrs R. E., Cushendall, County Antrim, 1962 (UFTM, Collector's Notebooks, Antrim (i), V 12).

[104] Sneddon, 'Witchcraft, Representation and Memory', p. 255.

south of the island, is needed to further explore the contours and extent of this belief. It is however unlikely that the teacher in a school in Cork in 1857 who asked the children in his class what a witch was would have received the same response had he mooted the same question to schoolchildren in 1957: nearly every boy in 1857 named a local witch and one of their victims.[105] This survey of belief in the supernatural in twentieth-century Ireland, in combination with earlier research on the eighteenth and nineteenth centuries, makes it difficult to apply the disenchanted thesis to the country, or to suggest it experienced a straightforward decline in witchcraft and magic. Indeed, the idea of the transformed, adaptive continuation of witchcraft belief may be further evidenced by recent, exciting research on witchcraft and Satanism and the rise of Irish Pagan witchcraft. Ironically, this section frames the next two sections of this Element, suggesting that modern representations (from journalists, antiquarians, historians, folklorists to poets, playwrights, and novelists) of historic witchcraft trials ignored the extent to which belief witchcraft permeated Irish society and culture in the past and in the present day.

3 Writing the History of Irish Witchcraft

British witchcraft historiography arguably began in the early eighteenth century. It examined early modern witch-hunting and explained its supposed decline at the end of the seventeenth century in rationalist, triumphalist terms. These Whiggish explorations were to some extent challenged in the early twentieth century by historians, such as Wallace Notestein, George Lyman Kittredge, and C. L'Estange Ewen, who based their conclusions on careful examination of surviving manuscripts and printed primary sources. Other early twentieth-century contributors, such as Margaret Murray and Sir James Frazer, asserted that early modern witchcraft was part of an ancient religion, while Montague Summers was convinced of the reality of the devil-worshipping witch. Later in the century, the legal, socio-economic, and political contexts in which accusations arose and trials were held was re-examined. Furthermore, the importance of gender was reassessed and witchcraft was located within a larger context of belief in a moral, magical universe populated with angels, demons, ghosts, familiar spirits, and cunning folk. Research conducted on witch trials in continental Europe, North America, and Scotland also began to shape how English witchcraft was viewed. As discussed in the previous section, historians also started to consider what happened to belief in

---

[105] *Cork Examiner*, 1 May 1857.

witches and witchcraft after the end of the witch trials in the eighteenth century.[106]

Jan Machielsen has recently re-examined the origins of witchcraft historiography to suggest that one of its main concerns, stretching back into the eighteenth century, was to assert that witchcraft was *history*, past-tense; a product of irrationality and superstition eventually corrected by scientific rationalism. Furthermore, he argues that through a close study of an overlooked contribution to academic witchcraft scholarship from the late nineteenth century, namely the work of American academic historians, George Lincoln Burr and Andrew Dickson White, insight can be gained into how personal and individual circumstances shape the writing of the history of witchcraft.[107] 'This study', he continues, 'will show that there is real value in taking stock and examining the longer history of our own field'.[108]

If, however, we are to fully understand 'the history of our own field', it is essential to move beyond Britain and America, and indeed Scotland,[109] and examine the unexplored witchcraft historiographies of other countries. If Burr and White's contribution to witchcraft historiography has been underappreciated, there has been almost no study of Irish historical writing on witchcraft.[110] This section will suggest that Irish witchcraft historiography developed along a different trajectory to the academic historiography of witch-hunting. From the early nineteenth century onwards, up until the late twentieth century, it was written by antiquarians, folklorists, and local and popular historians rather than by professional historians working out of university departments and writing for scholarly journals or academic publishers. This work was light on historical contextualisation (especially with regards witch-hunting in other countries), and even in the twentieth and twenty-first centuries, it did not follow academic conventions, with regards presentation, footnoting, or referencing. It was firmly based on primary-source evidence thanks largely to the efforts of demonologists, antiquarians, and historians, who, between the late seventeenth and late nineteenth centuries, transcribed, edited, and published material relating to Irish witchcraft and magic. Building on arguments first articulated in Ireland in the eighteenth century (see earlier in the

---

[106] Gaskill, 'Witchcraft Trials in England', pp. 283–9; Gaskill, 'Pursuit of Reality', pp. 1069–70; Davies, *America Bewitched*, pp. 2–4.

[107] Machielsen, *War on Witchcraft*, pp. 1–4, 6, 17, 21, 29–30, 43.

[108] Machielsen, *War on Witchcraft*, p. 10.

[109] Early modern Scottish witch trials first attracted the attention of scholars in the late eighteenth century. This historiography grew steadily during the nineteenth century: Gibson, *Rediscovering Renaissance Witchcraft*, p. 41; Sharpe, 'Witch-hunting and Witch Historiography', p. 183.

[110] For a brief examination of how local historians represented the Islandmagee trial in the nineteenth and early twentieth centuries: Sneddon, 'Witchcraft Belief, Representation and Memory', pp. 259–61.

text), early witchcraft historiography created a very powerful, influential narrative of Irish witchcraft. Firstly, Ireland was regarded as superior to the rest of Europe, as it had avoided large scale, early modern witch-hunting, which in its turn was explained by the fact that Irish people had never really believed in witchcraft. The few trials that did occur were explained-away as an aberration, the product of witch beliefs brought to Ireland from Scotland and England. These cases were nevertheless used in much the same way that British and American historians used their own witch trials: to distance themselves from the (perceived) irrationality and religious bigotry of the past that they believed witch-hunting epitomised. Secondly, no matter the period in which they were writing, Irish witchcraft historians erroneously portrayed present-day Ireland as disenchanted: that any residual belief in witchcraft had been long ejected as a serious concern for Irish people and thus held little social or cultural significance. Thirdly, historians gendered witchcraft and witches as female, and used carefully constructed representations of the accused witches to articulate and maintain patriarchal gender norms. It was only in the very late twentieth century that professional, university-based studies of Irish witchcraft began to challenge these narratives.

Laying the Foundations: Original Documents

One of the problems of studying Irish witchcraft and popular magic in the past is that many of the records which are the staple sources for historians studying witchcraft in Britain, Europe, and in America were lost in fires in the seventeenth and eighteenth centuries, or in the destruction of the Public Record Office in Dublin in 1922 during the Irish Civil War. This included probate material, parish and institutional manuscripts relating to the Established Church of Ireland, and administrative and criminal court records.[111] This loss has been compensated to some extent by the fact that demonologists, antiquarians, and 'gentlemen scholar' historians began, relatively early on, publishing primary material relating to salient Irish witchcraft cases. This began with the publication, in the late seventeenth century, of an edited version of documents relating to Florence Newton's trial in 1661. Primary-source material relating to the Islandmagee trial was published in the eighteenth and nineteenth centuries, while key documents relating to the Dame Alice Kyteler case were published in the 1840s. On the other hand, manuscript material relating to the Mary Butters case was not published until the late twentieth century. As this section and the next will show, the influence of these publications on later Irish historians, journalists, playwrights, and poets is difficult to underestimate. Irish

---

[111] Edwards and O'Dowd, *Sources for Modern Irish History*, pp. 131–8; Garnham, 'Local Elite Creation', p. 624.

published primary sources thus worked in a similar manner to Scottish 'legal historical works' of the late eighteenth and nineteenth centuries that provided 'the crucial access to original records ... which creative writers found so fascinating in later times'.[112]

Up until the twenty-first century, historians wishing to study the trial of Florence Newton in Cork in September 1661 relied on various editions of English philosopher, writer, and clergyman Joseph Glanvill in his, *Saducismus Triumphatus*, the first edition of which appeared in 1681. *Saducismus Triumphatus* was edited and published a year after Glanvill's death by his associate and fellow clergyman, Henry More. It was an ideologically charged book that is often regarded as a seminal work in the canon of anti-Sadducee demonology that appeared in Britain and America from the late seventeenth century. Anti-Saduccee, demonological literature marshalled narratives on ghosts, witchcraft, and demonic possession to act as empirical proof of the existence of the spirit world, and by extrapolation, of God, to challenge 'atheists' who portrayed the universe in mechanistic and materialist terms.[113] Demonologists of Glanvill's stamp ensured the cases they detailed appeared to be based on verifiable evidence, otherwise they could not be regarded as empirical proof of the supernatural. Thus the 'relation' or account of the Youghal 1661 trial included in *Saducismus Triumphatus* was purported to be 'taken out of a copy of an Authentick Record, as I conceive, every half sheet having W. Aston writ in the margin, and then again W. Aston at the end of all, who in all likelihood must be some publick Notary, or Record-Keeper'.[114] In reality, it was a shorter, edited, re-structured version of a transcript of witness testimonies noted down at Newton's trial and signed by the presiding Judge, Sir William Aston. These documents were preserved in the Boyle papers in the Royal Society in London and were eventually transcribed and published in 2019.[115] Historians of the witch lynching in Antrim in 1698 were similarly reliant on posthumously published editions (appearing after 1696) of another anti-Sadducee text, George Sinclair's *Satan's Invisible World Discovered ...* (1685), until the rediscovery in the twenty-first century of the original, anonymous pamphlet account: Daniel Higgs, *The Wonderful and True Relation of the*

---

[112] Gibson, *Rediscovering Renaissance Witchcraft*, p. 44.

[113] Sneddon, 'Florence Newton's Trial', pp. 299–300. For a discussion of this demonology: Cameron, *Enchanted Europe*, pp. 270–85. Jonathan Barry however warns against homogenising, under the banner of Anti-Saduccee, late seventeenth-century anthologies of the supernatural, on the grounds that they were written by authors from extremely disparate backgrounds with diverse political and religious concerns and motivations: Barry, 'News from the Invisible World', pp. 184–8.

[114] Glanvill, *Saducismus Triumphatus*, p. 386.

[115] See, Sneddon, 'Florence Newton's Trial', pp. 306–19.

Bewitching of a Young Girle in Ireland, What Ways she was Tormented, and a Receipt of the Ointment that she was Cured with (1699).[116]

The trial of the Islandmagee witches in 1711 has fascinated generations of historians, journalists, and writers largely because, by the end of the nineteenth century an unusually large amount of important manuscript material relating to the case was preserved and made widely accessible. Between 1650 and 1750, Irish history writing was no longer circulated in manuscript in Irish but published in English by Protestant authors drawn from the gentry. These historians wrote primarily for men of similar backgrounds and means but there was some market for cheaper, popular histories. The historiographical trends of Gaelic scholarship, particularly annalistic chronicling, were traded in for narratives infused with religious, moral, or political purpose. Partisan Protestant readings of the upheavals of the seventeenth century were particularly prominent. Memoirs and correspondence of leading political personages involved in these events, which were usually edited by family members, were also popular and formed the basis on which future narratives could be built. It nevertheless remained easier to write than publish Irish history in this period. Authors of more limited means had to raise subscriptions to cover the cost of printing, while a small number circulated their work in manuscript. The situation changed somewhat in the late 1700s, as readers of Irish history grew along with numbers of Irish printers, booksellers, readers, and libraries. Along with a healthy trade in pirated editions of English history books, notable works of Irish history were published in Dublin that aimed to provide Ireland with a grand narrative that encompassed settler and native history while not avoiding the tumults of the seventeenth century. This Protestant, historiographical hegemony was challenged by a number of histories of native Ireland that although written in English were founded upon antiquarian scholarship that utilised pre-conquest archives. Irish antiquarian scholarship was given a further lift in the last decades of the century by the launch of learned, illustrated journals and the establishment, under charter, of the Royal Irish Academy in Dublin in 1785.[117] In the first three decades of the nineteenth century, history writing dealing with modern Ireland was unashamedly political and presentist, and offered little new by way of presentation or sources used. In contrast, works dedicated to legal, topographical, and ancient

---

[116] Seymour, *Irish Witchcraft and Demonology*, pp. 194–7; Crone, 'Witchcraft in Antrim', pp. 34–5; Sneddon, 'Medicine, Belief, Witchcraft'. For Sinclair: Craik, 'Hydrostatical Works of George Sinclair', pp. 239–73; Bath and Newton, 'Sensible Proof of Spirits', pp. 1–14. One of the few extant copies of Higgs' *Wonderful and True Relation* can be found in the Ferguson collection, University of Glasgow.

[117] Gillespie and Hadfield, *Irish Book, 1550–1800*, chapters 14–16; Barnard, 'Histories', pp. 96–8.

history were increasingly based on authentic sources; an endeavour helped by the foundation of further learned societies.[118] Irish developments were matched in the eighteenth and nineteenth centuries by a wider, preservation and access-driven vogue for publishing historical records. In the eighteenth century, this work was carried out by men working in the antiquarian tradition who were concerned primarily with textual remains rather than writing history themselves.[119]

The publication of the first primary source relating to the Islandmagee trial (a long, private letter written by Dr William Tisdall that detailed the events he had witnessed on 31 March 1711) can be placed firmly within this antiquarian tradition. It was printed without introduction or explanation in the January 1775 edition of the literary periodical, *Hibernian Magazine*.[120] Tisdall was a High-Church Tory vicar of Belfast and owned property in Carrickfergus.[121] In 1822, Tisdall's letter was supplemented by the publication of a lengthy, extremely detailed pamphlet account of events leading up to the trial which had been written in late 1711 by an anonymous chronicler. The pamphlet was edited, transcribed, and published by self-educated, Carrickfergus grocer, antiquarian and historian, Samuel McSkimin. Although McSkimin was in regular contact with contemporary antiquarians, he did not join a learned society, and he not only collected and edited original documents but used them as sources in his books and articles on local history.[122] In the century before publication, the manuscript version of the pamphlet was circulated in much the same way as earlier manuscript histories had been. McSkimin's published version contained a brief description of the apprehension and conviction of the ninth Islandmagee 'witch', William Sellor, and a copy of the Tisdall letter, reproduced verbatim from the *Hibernian Magazine*.[123] In 1896, Robert Magill Young, architect and archaeologist, edited and published the pre-trial depositions of witnesses, including the testimony of Mary Dunbar, recorded in early 1711 by Justice of the Peace and Mayor of Carrickfergus, Edward Clements.[124] Young based this publication on transcriptions made in the 1860s by William Pinkerton, a Belfast-based antiquarian and historian, from original manuscripts housed (where they still are kept) in Trinity College, Dublin.[125] Tisdall's letter and the manuscript version of the pamphlet account have since been lost.

---

[118] MacCartney, 'History in Ireland'.   [119] Riordan, 'Materials for History', pp. 51–77.

[120] Tisdall, 'Account of the Trial of Eight Reputed Witches', pp. 47–51.

[121] Hayton, *Ruling Ireland*, p. 202.   [122] Williams, 'McSkimin'.

[123] McSkimin, *Islandmagee Witches*; Sneddon, 'Witchcraft, Representation and Memory', p. 9.

[124] Young, *Historical Notes*, pp. 161–4.

[125] 'Examinations and Depositions taken in the Co. Antrim Respecting Witches', March 1711 (TCD, Samuel Molyneux Papers, Ms 883/2, pp. 273–85); William Pinkerton to George Benn,

Primary-source material relating to the Mary Butters case remained unpub-lished and inaccessible to only the most hardened researchers until the late twentieth century. The original court documents and coroner records were presumably lost in 1922. Luckily, full details of the inquest held at Carnmoney on 19 August 1807 into the deaths of Margaret Lee, Elizabeth and David Montgomery, as well as the criminal proceedings that followed, were reported in contemporary newspapers.[126] More detailed descriptions of the case, based on local knowledge and oral tradition, were provided by compliers of the OSMI in early 1839,[127] but these were not published until the 1990s.[128] In 1862, William Orr McGaw, who was born in Carnmoney in 1798, combined newspaper reports with oral tradition and personal memory to produce an even more detailed narrative of the case. This revealed that Butters had been threatened and assaulted by local people after the discovery of the bodies in the Montgomery house. McGaw's narrative was largely unknown until its publication in 1955.[129]

Writing the History of Irish Witchcraft: The Nineteenth Century

In Ireland in the 1830s, the study of the Irish past was divided between those wishing carry on the antiquarian scholarship of the previous century and those influenced by Victorian utilitarianism. The latter employed new methodologies, showed respect for the Irish language and manuscripts, and tried to steer a course between those histories which romanticised Ireland's past or wrote it solely from the perspective of settlers and conquerors. In 1851, John O'Donovan published his landmark, *Annals of the Kingdom of Ireland by the Four Masters*, an edition in Gaelic and English translation of *Annála Ríoghachta Éireann* which had been compiled from early manuscript sources. The nineteenth century also saw the publication of numerous popular histories, biographies and papers of prominent political figures. Taken as a whole, history

---

16 March 1868 (PRONI, Benn Papers, D3113/7/149); Sneddon, 'Witchcraft, Representation and Memory', p. 9.

[126] *BNL*, 21 August 1807; *Caledonian Mercury*, 24 August 1807; *BNL*, 15 April 1808; *Hibernian Journal; or, Chronicle of Liberty*, 15 April 1808. The report from 21 August 1807 was partly transcribed by an unknown author, possibly George Benn, nineteenth-century historian of Belfast: 'Account of Unsuccessful Attempt at Witchcraft in Carnmoney, August 1807', n.d. (PRONI, Benn Papers, D3113/7/237). The hostility of the author to popular magic is implied by the fact that he described Butters' un-witching activities as 'witchcraft'. The *BNL* report from 21 August 1807 was reproduced 150 years later in a feature article: 'Today Long Ago'', *BT*, 18 August 1958. For a similar article published for the 100-year anniversary: 'A Century Ago', *BNL*, 21 August 1907.

[127] 'Fair Sheets', 1839, pp. 23, 34–8.   [128] OSMI, ii, pp. 75–6.

[129] McGaw, 'Tragic Occurrence', pp. 113–15. McGaw's notes on wider belief in witchcraft and fairies in Protestant Carnmoney can be found here: McGaw, 'Notes on the Parish of Carnmoney', pp. 53–7.

writing in nineteenth-century Ireland was informed by specific religious and political viewpoints which were increasingly polarised across Roman Catholic Nationalist and Protestant Unionist lines. History books were often written in response to present political controversies, to counter the 'propaganda' of other historical works, or to provide a narrative palatable to an intended audience.[130]

In keeping with broader historiographical trends, from the nineteenth century onwards Irish local historians and folklorists began to use published archival material to produce narrative accounts (published in periodicals and books) of the cases focused on in this Element. These cases were regarded by the largely Protestant historians who documented them as isolated incidents that stained Ireland's otherwise clean record with regards witch-hunting. This disenchanted past was linked to a disenchanted present, free of belief in witchcraft. Witches and witch trials were also feminised, and witches repositioned as the pious, innocent victims of a bigoted, irrational legal system, over which they had no control. This gendered reading of Irish witchcraft obscured the agency and resistance shown by some Irish witches to the prosecution and trial process.

The pioneer of Irish folklore, Thomas Crofton Croker published his first collection of oral folk tales in 1824, *Researches in the South of Ireland*, which contained lengthy sections on death customs and supernatural agency. His next book, *Fairy Legends and Traditions of the South of Ireland*, was published in three volumes between 1825 and 1828, and was based on legends and short narratives concerning the supernatural rather than detailed folk tales. Croker, a Protestant, was criticised by later historians for exploiting Irish material to sell to an English audience, employing stereotypical images of the Irish 'peasantry', and linking their 'superstitions' to their Roman Catholic faith.[131] In common with most early Irish historians of witchcraft, irrespective of their religious or political stamp, he was influenced by eighteenth-century enlightenment rhetoric. Ireland had, thankfully in his opinion, avoided the witch-hunting stage in its national evolution, unlike its close its neighbours in Britain. Furthermore, any outbreaks of witch-hunting that occurred in Ireland were the product of cultural infection, brought into the country by outsiders, namely English and Scottish settlers. In April 1833, Croker, in a letter to the editor of the *Dublin Penny Journal* (co-founded in 1832 by antiquarian George Petrie) suggested that Kilkenny 'was particularly fatal to witches' in light of the Kyteler case of 1324. He went onto state that 'Ireland has been, in my opinion, unjustly stigmatised as a barbarous and superstitious country – it is certain that the

---

[130] Murphy, *Irish Book, 1800–1891*, chapters 39–41.

[131] Ó Gio’lláin, *Locating Irish Folklore*, pp. 94–10; for a forceful criticism of Croker's anti-Catholicism and lack of knowledge and understanding of Irish history, language, and antiquities: MacCarthy, 'Croker'.

cruel persecution carried on against poor and ignorant old women was as nothing in Ireland when compared with other countries'. The Kilkenny execution, he continued, took place in 'a town, the inhabitants of which were almost entirely either English settlers or of English descent'. The 'one other execution for the crime of witchcraft' he contended 'took place at Antrim, in 1699 . . . The particulars of this silly tragedy were printed in a pamphlet, entitled "The bewitching of a child in Ireland, and from thence copied by Professor Sinclair."'[132] As has already been established, both cases were not in fact witchcraft trials. Croker advised the people of Kilkenny to 'not be ashamed of' the Kilkenny case, for it was a solitary event that occurred a long time ago. Scotland on the other hand was executing witches up until the eighteenth century, while in contemporary England many people still believed in witchcraft. No mention was made of continuing belief closer to home.[133] Although of a very different religious and political stamp, Peter Finlay, writing in the Jesuit-founded *Irish Monthly* in 1874, was of the much same mind as Croker. He stated that Ireland was witchcraft trial free with the exceptions of the Kyteler and Islandmagee cases: 'it is worthy of remark that in neither case were the accusers or accused of Irish origin'.[134]

Joseph Glanvill's *Saducismus Triumphatus* introduced the Youghal trial to numerous scholars writing for nineteenth-century British and Irish periodicals. A particularly intemperate Irish Protestant, writing for the *Dublin University Magazine* in 1847, stated that even Catholic 'Irishmen (at least nowadays) are too religious' to believe in witchcraft, and were thus less superstitious than the Protestants of Youghal who accused Newton of witchcraft.[135] The *Dublin University Magazine* was a popular Protestant periodical published monthly between 1833 and 1877, and offered increasingly rich pickings for those interested in the supernatural.[136] Nineteenth-century British writers who wrote about the Youghal trial did not attempt to explain it away, nor did they laud Ireland for avoiding the ravages of the witch-hunts.[137] One however used the 'pseudo-science' of mesmerism to explain Newton's apparent magical powers. Mesmerism grew out of the theories and practices of Franz Anton Mesmer in the late eighteenth century and experienced a revival in England in the 1830s and 1840s, as both a medical practice and a popular entertainment. It

---

[132] Croker, 'Witchcraft in Kilkenny', p. 341. This murder/lynching was committed in 1698, not in 1699.

[133] Croker, 'Witchcraft in Kilkenny', p. 341.

[134] Finlay, 'Witchcraft', 1874, p. 525. For the association of witch-hunts with Protestant monarchs such as James VI of Scotland, see p. 527.

[135] 'Another Evening with the Witchfinders', pp. 146–61 (quote at p. 152).

[136] Tilley, 'Periodicals', pp. 154–9; Hall, *Dialogues in the Margin*.

[137] I. P., 'Rise and Progress of Witchcraft', pp. 581–2; Wood, 'Witchcraft', p. 655.

was eventually eclipsed in the 1850s by Spiritualism. Mesmerists put their subjects into mesmeric trances by staring into their eyes, or by making sweeping movements over their bodies. They claimed that the trance was achieved by transmitting forces and fluids from their own bodies, or from inanimate substances, to that of the subject.[138] Thus, in 1824, a writer for *Chambers' Edinburgh Journal* was able to suggest that mesmerism explained why Newton was able to cause Longdon to experience a convulsive fit, across an open courtroom, merely by looking at her and waving her hands in the air:

> In the case of Florence Newton, tried at Youghal in 1661, one of the practices of the mesmerists is precisely described. It is stated that, during the trial, when the accuser had closed her evidence, the prisoner looked at her, and made motions of her hands towards her, upon which she immediately fell into fits so violent, that all the people lay hands upon her could not hold her.[139]

Samuel McSkimin's interest in the Islandmagee witches began in 1809 when he devoted a few lines to the case in a Belfast periodical, stating that the trial took place 'during the reign of superstition', and that 'at present superstition is no trait in the character of the people of Island Magee'.[140] This was of course far from the truth. Belief in witchcraft remained strong in Islandmagee up until the twentieth century, reinforced by the social memory and trauma of the 1711 trial.[141] Donald Harmon Akenson's exceptionally well written, researched, and referenced local history, *Between Two Revolutions, Islandmagee, County Antrim, 1798–1920* (1978), covered every aspect of the peninsula in the long nineteenth century, including continued belief in fairies, ghosts, the Devil, magical healing, and apotropaic magic.[142] McSkimin published his first, full article on the Islandmagee case in 1818, in which he detailed the trial of the eight women, their sentence (which he assured readers 'was fully executed'), and the fact that, 'William Sellor, husband of … Janet Sellor, was also tried at the following assizes for the like offences, and also, found guilty'.[143] McSkimin's major contribution to the history of the Islandmagee witches came with the publication of his successful and influential work, *The History and Antiquities of the County of the Town of Carrickfergus, Co. Antrim*. This was first published by subscription in 1811, with enlarged editions appearing in 1823 and in 1829. Addenda were added to the book in 1833, while an appendix and illustrations

---

[138] Bell, *Magical Imagination*, pp. 82–3, 150–1; Melechi, *Servants of the Supernatural*, pp. 7–76; Owen, *Darkened Room*, pp. 20, 109; Winter, *Mesmerised*, pp. 1–4.

[139] 'A New Explanation of Old Superstitions', pp. 382–3.

[140] S. M. S., 'Account of Island Magee, 1809', p. 105.

[141] Sneddon, 'Witchcraft, Representation and Memory', pp. 255–8.

[142] Akenson, *Two Revolutions*, pp. 55, 135–7, 142–3.

[143] S. M. S., 'Statistical Account of Island Magee', p. 510.

appeared in the 1839 edition.[144] In the first edition, McSkimin dedicated just over a page to the events leading up to the trial and to the trial itself. He also included a description of the accused women: 'In the defence of the accused, it appeared they were all honest, industrious people; that they received the communion, and generally prayed both in public and private'.[145] In the second, expanded edition, in which a longer account of the trial was provided, no mention was made of William Sellor, and an enduring myth was introduced, for which there is no evidentiary basis, that one of the convicted women lost an eye while being pilloried in Carrickfergus as part of her sentence: 'these unfortunate people ... were severely pelted in the pillory, with boiled eggs, cabbage stalks and the like, by which one of them had an eye beaten out'.[146]

McSkimin excluded William Sellor from various editions of his book because his involvement derailed his main argument that the Islandmagee witches were good women (as measured against patriarchal standards of the day) victimised by an irrational and superstitious society. McSkimin based his description of the women on a selective and unproblematic reading of William Tisdall's letter from 1711, which gave a highly partisan account of the trial. Tisdall was vehemently anti-Presbyterian and anti-Whig, and so was unwilling to support a witchcraft accusation supported by these factions in Co. Antrim. In the letter, Tisdall, adopted a two-pronged approach to undermine the conviction of the Islandmagee witches. First, he argued that Dunbar's symptoms were the product of illusory visions placed in her mind by the Devil so that innocent people could be convicted of witchcraft. Secondly, he suggested that the majority of the Islandmagee witches were not the type of people that the Devil usually recruited to his ranks: they were innocent, pious, respectable, sober, and churchgoing.[147] This is however not the view of the women that arises from the pamphlet account or pre-trial depositions. Indeed, the convicted women were rendered believable witches in the eyes of their neighbours and prosecutors precisely because they challenged gender norms in the way they looked, spoke, and behaved. Most of them did not conform to male views of feminine beauty, through old age, illness, physical impairment, or disfigurement. Some were described as 'dirty' looking, uneducated, or prone to fits of rage. They swore, drank alcohol, and one, Catherine McCalmond, was said to be of an 'ill fame'. More importantly, they resisted the male legal system at every turn. On the day of the trial, 31 March 1711, all the women pled not guilty,

[144] Carson, 'McSkimin'.

[145] McSkimin, *History and Antiquities of Carrickfergus*, 1811, pp. 21–2 (quote at p. 22).

[146] McSkimin, *History and Antiquities of Carrickfergus*, 1823, pp. 72–4 (quote at p. 74).

[147] Sneddon, 'Witchcraft, Representation and Memory', pp. 9–10.

and at various times during the initial investigation they obstructed the prosecution process, by challenging Dunbar's version of events, and through non-compliance: from refusing to be interviewed by magistrates and constables, to resisting arrest.[148] Two of the accused, Janet Carson and Janet Main, were aided in their resistance by family members. Carson's daughter unsuccessfully appealed to Revd Robert Sinclair, Presbyterian minister of Islandmagee, to have her mother's name cleared,[149] while Main's husband, Andrew Ferguson, objected to the way a crude identity parade, from which his wife had been picked by Dunbar, had been organised.[150] It was not unusual in early modern European witch trials (including those held in Scotland and England) for family members (husbands, parents, and even children) to support and defend immediate kin accused of witchcraft, especially mothers and wives.[151]

McSkimin's influence on the way Irish historians viewed the Islandmagee witch trial was almost immediate. In 1833, Robert Young, father of antiquarian R.M. Young (publisher of the Islandmagee depositions) argued that Ireland had not been bothered by witch trials until the witch-hunting Scots came to Ulster, and suggested that the Islandmagee witches were sober, industrious, church-going victims of popular bigotry.[152] McSkimin's influence also stretched across the Irish Sea. English antiquarian and journalist, Thomas Wright ended his book on medieval and early modern sorcery and magic with a lengthy description of the Islandmagee case based on McSkimin's edition of the 1711 pamphlet account. Wright paid particular attention to the sorcery used by the 'witches' to summon the demons who attacked Knowehead House and possessed Mary Dunbar. He ended his book with the Islandmagee case because he believed that it marked the juncture at which 'sorcery and magic' no longer held a 'place in the history of mankind', when rationalism conquered first the culture of the educated and then that of the 'vulgar'.[153] If McSkimin brought the Islandmagee trial to a wider audience by publishing the 1711 pamphlet, Wright's edition of *The Narrative of the Proceedings against Dame Alice Kyteler*, published in

---

[148] Sneddon, *Possessed by the Devil*.

[149] McSkimin, *Islandmagee Witches*, pp. 9–10 (quote at p. 10).

[150] Deposition of Hugh Wilson, 10 March 1711 (TCD, Molyneux Papers, Ms 883/2, p. 278); McSkimin, *Islandmagee* Witches, pp. 9, 14, 16–17.

[151] Briggs, *Witches and Neighbours,* p. 197; Gaskill, *Crime and Mentalities*, pp. 51–2; Martin, 'Witchcraft and Family', p. 15.

[152] Young, 'Carrickfergus', pp. 369–71 (quote at p. 370). Young made notes on Tisdall's letter published in the *Hibernian Magazine*: 'Ms Note of 8 Supposed Witches Accused of Tormenting Young Gentlewoman, Mary Dunbar', n.d. (PRONI, Young Family Papers, D2930/4/81).

[153] Wright, *Narratives of Sorcery and Magic*, pp. 336–41, 417–20 (quote at p. 342). Wright knew Thomas Crofton Croker and published an edition of his *Fairy Legends and Traditions of the South of Ireland* in 1862: Thomas Wright to Thomas Crofton Croker, 12 December 1843 (British Library, Western Manuscripts, Loan 96 RLF 1/769/18); Thompson, 'Wright, Thomas (1810–1877)'.

London in 1843, did the same for the Kyteler case. The *Narrative*, currently held in the British Library, was a Latin manuscript copy of the now lost original manuscript written by Ledrede in the fourteenth century.[154]

If the Newton, Kyteler, and Islandmagee cases drew the attention of numerous nineteenth-century scholars and historians, the trial of Mary Butters was largely overlooked.[155] This is unsurprising given the fact that historians in that period were unlikely to come across the case unless they had an intimate knowledge of early nineteenth-century Belfast newspapers. Its omission by Samuel McSkimin from various editions of his *History of Carrickfergus* is perhaps harder to explain given that both he and Butters lived in Carrickfergus at the same time and his correspondence with Thomas Crofton Croker demonstrates that he was aware of the case.[156] McSkimin also discussed the case in 1839 in person with researchers for the OSMI.[157] McSkimin perhaps found it uncomfortable to write of an incident that had occurred in his beloved town and which cast it an unflattering light. An enlarged edition of the book, published posthumously as 'a labour of love' in 1909 by his great grand-daughter, Elizabeth J. McCrum, however included a lengthy 'note' on the prosecution of Mary Butters.[158]

Writing the History of Irish Witchcraft: The Late Nineteenth and Twentieth Centuries

From the late nineteenth century to the late twentieth century, Irish witchcraft history continued to be written by those working outside of academic history. Their popular narratives, anthologies and local histories were now published in books rather than in periodicals, but they nevertheless betrayed the ideological concerns of their predecessors. Although lacking footnotes, bibliographies, and wider historical contextualisation, they were based on oral tradition and printed primary sources. Dixon Donaldson, headmaster, local personality, and author of a privately printed, local history of Islandmagee, first published in 1927, opened his account of 'The Islandmagee Witches', with words that could have been written in 1827: 'Living in an age happily sceptical of the superstitious beliefs of our ancestors, it may not be uninteresting to present a brief account of the history of witchcraft and its kindred arts before going into the details of the notorious case that occurred in this district in the year 1711'.[159] He went onto state that 'Belief in witchcraft and sorcery seems to have been universally

---

[154] Wright, *Dame Alice Kyteler*; Callan, *Templars, the Witch, and the Wild Irish*, pp. 79–80, 82.
[155] It is mentioned very briefly, along with the Islandmagee trial, in an article published in the *Dublin University Magazine* in 1873: M. S. H., 'Witchcraft in Ireland', pp. 218–23.
[156] Young, *Historical Notes*, p. 267.   [157] 'Fair Sheets', 1839, pp. 23, 37.
[158] McCrum, *Carrickfergus*, p. 101.   [159] Donaldson, *History of Islandmagee*, p. 43.

associated with religious superstitions throughout the ages'.[160] The account of early modern witch-hunting that followed contained numerous factual errors. James I was, for example charged with bringing draconian witchcraft laws to England and Scotland and accused of making it legal to torture for a confession in both jurisdictions. Donaldson also claimed that during the time of the Long Parliament (1640–1) 3000 witches 'mainly from the defenceless classes of the poor and aged', were executed in England when in fact the number was closer to 500. Europe, Dixon noted, was only released from the spell of witch-hunting in the early eighteenth century, where 'the spread of popular education and the consequent release of democratic privileges in the nineteenth century have been responsible for the general disappearance of many of the superstitious beliefs that were a stumbling block to the peace of mind and the social welfare of our ancestors'. His treatment of the Islandmagee trial however was based on evidence gleaned from Tisdall's letter, Young's printed depositions, and the pamphlet account. He supplemented this material with oral testimony, or as he put it, with 'accounts handed down by word of mouth even to the present generation'.[161] As a result, he was able to produce a very detailed description of events before, during, and after the trial, which drew on extensive knowledge of local architecture and the personal histories of trial witnesses and deponents. He was also one of the few historians to detail the apprehension and trial of William Sellor.[162]

Some books on Irish witchcraft published between the late nineteenth and late twentieth centuries were less concerned with local history and more with the entertainment value of the few 'witchcraft' cases that Ireland afforded. These works were well written, readable, inexpensive, and widely available and had a significant influence in shaping perceptions of Irish witchcraft. Classon Porter, non-subscribing minister of Larne, local historian and biographer, wrote a series of articles on Ulster's ghosts and witchcraft trials for the *Northern Whig* newspaper which were then reprinted in book form as, *Witches, Warlocks and Ghosts* (1885). The book was written to entertain and inform the general reader and was structured as an anthology. A large proportion of it was given over to a lengthy and detailed description of the Islandmagee trial based on McSkimin's edition of the pamphlet account. The inclusion of the lost-eye myth, along with the exclusion of William Sellor, makes one suspect that McSkimin's *History of Carrickfergus* was also close to hand.[163] Porter's handling of the 1698 Antrim case was particularly interesting. In common with earlier historians, he was unable to lay his hands on a copy of the 1699 pamphlet

---

[160] Donaldson, *History of Islandmagee*, p. 43. [161] Donaldson, *History of Islandmagee*, p. 44.

[162] Donaldson, *History of Islandmagee*, pp. 44–8.

[163] Porter, *Witches, Warlocks and Ghosts*, pp. 1–12.

account, and instead used George Sinclair's book to produce a concise but detailed account of the case.[164] Unlike other authors, his narrative was also informed by local tradition, 'lingering' about Antrim town. This oral tradition painted a very different picture of the case. It suggested that the old woman who bewitched the young girl had, by 1698, a long-standing reputation for practising witchcraft and had been driven from her home as a result. At the time of her accusation, she was said to have been living in a cave in a field near to the Antrim Presbyterian meeting house. It was here that she was tracked down by neighbours, stabbed to death, and her body cut into pieces which were then scattered about the town.[165] Porter believed this version above that given by Sinclair in his book, which he stated, 'would lead us to think that the unfortunate woman, before being put to death, was tried and condemned by some legal authority'. Porter continued, 'If there was any law at all in this case it was the law which is administered and executed by Judge Lynch'.[166]

Porter's anthology set the tone for later books, with regards intended audience, presentation, and a lack of engagement with scholarly work on witch trials in early modern Scotland, England, North America, or on the continent. Patrick Byrne's *Witchcraft in Ireland*, first published in 1967, stretched the definition of 'witch' to include the cases of Alice Kyteler, Mary Butters, and Bridget Cleary, who was murdered by her husband and accomplices in 1895 in Co. Tipperary as a suspected fairy changeling. Contemporary newspapers however had reported the case as a 'witch burning'. Byrne's book also covered the trials of Florence Newton and the Islandmagee witches, and followed Porter's lead by suggesting that the 1698 case was a lynching.[167] Bob Curran's 2005 book, *A Bewitched Land*, was similar in structure, style and layout but took a more complex view of Irish witchcraft, as it was informed by an early twentieth-century book, St. John Drelincourt Seymour's *Irish Witchcraft and Demonology* (1913) and various (unreferenced) scholarly texts written in the 1970s. Curran's book was clearly influenced by the charity-refused model formulated by Keith Thomas and Alan Macfarlane. This model placed social tensions, experienced in close-knit communities under social and economic transition, at the heart of English witchcraft accusations. Curran's portrayal of witch-hunting as political and gender struggle was influenced by the work of Deirdre English and Barbara Ehrenreich. Curran regarded British witchcraft (which he also referred to as English witchcraft) as different to Continental witchcraft (which included Scotland), in that

---

[164] Porter, *Witches, Warlocks and Ghosts*, pp. 17–18.

[165] Porter, *Witches, Warlocks and Ghosts*, pp. 18–19.

[166] Porter, *Witches, Warlocks and Ghosts*, p. 19.

[167] See, Byrne, *Witchcraft in Ireland*, pp. 18–26, 51–5, 56–8, 28–35, 36–7, 38–46. For the Cleary case: Bourke, *Bridget Cleary*.

European witchcraft was demonically inspired and accusations and prosecutions came from 'above', from religious and political elites.[168] The 'figure of the Irish witch', Curran contended, had 'a number of functions (midwife, healer, mischief work)', and the distinctively Irish version of witchcraft was rooted in British and Continental beliefs as well as 'widespread Irish vernacular belief in fairies'.[169] Curran did not suggest that Ireland was witchcraft free, only that witch trials appeared in 'heavily Anglicised places', where British and Continental ideas had purchase, and where the healing and divination activities of outspoken and troublesome women were interpreted by male legal and clerical authorities as demonic[170]: the Alice Kyteler case was regarded as the product of Anglo-Norman settlement; the Youghal trial was seen as a typical English witch trial transported to Ireland by Puritans; and the Islandmagee case represented a combination of English village witchcraft and the demonism of continental Calvinism brought to Ulster by Presbyterian Scots. Mary Butters' case was relegated to the status of folk tale and placed at the back of the book.[171]

The study of Irish witchcraft by professional (if not academic) historians is often traced to Seymour's *Irish Witchcraft and Demonology*. Seymour combined scholarship on church and literary history with his day job as a Church of Ireland clergyman. In a biographical essay on Seymour, T. C. Barnard noted that his book on witchcraft was based on 'the latest literature from France and America' and that 'his handling was firmly anchored in the evidence'. He further commended him for comparing 'Ireland, with its seeming rarity of formal witchcraft accusations and prosecutions, with the different situations elsewhere in Europe and North America ... feeling his way towards an explanation of witchcraft as culturally as well as socially and economically determined'.[172] All this is true of course, as was the fact that Seymour built his book on extensive research conducted on a wide range of manuscript and printed primary-source material (including the sources detailed earlier in this section), which he referenced in footnotes, if neither systematically nor rigorously. It is crucial however not to overplay the novelty of Seymour's work, as it had much in common with earlier works. It was after all, in essence, a narrative history of salient cases of witchcraft, demonic and ghost activity. In his enumeration of witchcraft prosecution, he included the Kyteler heresy case, the 1698 lynching, and the Mary Butters prosecution, along with trials of Florence Newton and the Islandmagee witches (replete with a rendition of McSkimin's lost-eye myth and his exclusion of William Sellor). Seymour also suggested that

---

[168] Curran, *Bewitched Land*, pp. 7–13, 39–43.   [169] Curran, *Bewitched Land*, p. 14.

[170] Curran, *Bewitched Land*, pp. 9–12.

[171] Curran, *Bewitched Land*, pp. 14, 19–35, 39–59, 60–79, 80–116, 117–36, 137–50, 185–9.

[172] Barnard, 'Seymour'.

Irish witchcraft was limited to Protestant settler areas, and largely overlooked the witch beliefs of the majority, Gaelic-speaking, native Irish population. Although Seymour noted the prominence of butter- and milk-stealing magic in Gaelic-Irish culture (which he believed arrived in Ireland from Scandinavia in the Middle Ages), he did not regard this as a coherent body of witch beliefs but an instance of magical superstition in common with pishogues, magical healing and protective magic. He admitted that belief in witches that stole milk and butter and harmed humans had 'survived' into the twentieth century, and that these had occasionally led to criminal prosecutions, but explained them away as folklore, rural superstition, or the product of insanity. These beliefs, he argued, were far removed from the harmful magic, demonic worship, pacts, and Sabbats that marked early modern witchcraft. In Seymour's view, modern Ireland simply did not believe in this type of witch, unlike (he was pleased to report) early twentieth-century, rural England.[173] A contemporary reviewer of Seymour's book was more ambiguous about a disenchanted Ireland. He remarked that only under-employed curates such as Seymour had the time to write a book on witchcraft, a matter which, 'most of us simply put ... aside as unworthy of the consideration of sensible men' even if there are 'still people ... who say that they believe in witches'.[174] Other reviewers attacked the book's lack of engagement with Gaelic-Irish witchcraft and with sources written in Irish.[175] The book however was well received by the reading public, especially educated, urban Protestants.[176]

Modern Irish historiography is often traced to 1936 and the foundation of the *Ulster Society for Irish Historical Studies* in Belfast and the *Irish Historical Society* in Dublin. In 1938, they began to jointly publish the academic journal, *Irish Historical Studies* (*IHS*). The professional, objective history they promoted aimed to challenge and revise mythology and politically partisan history, and to move the subject further away from an antiquarian, fact-gathering approach. Their new history was to be dispassionate and founded on archival research and positivistic, 'scientific principles' to ensure it met the academic and professional standards comparable with scholarship elsewhere, especially Britain and Germany. Papers submitted to *IHS* thus had to follow austere

---

[173] Seymour, *Irish Witchcraft and Demonology*, chapters 1–3, 5, 8–9.

[174] *IT*, 3 October 1913. A similar review of Seymour's book, albeit containing anti-English sentiment, appeared in: Moutray Read, 'Review of *Irish Witchcraft and Demonology*', pp. - 322–3 and, 'Review of *Irish Witchcraft and Demonology*', pp. 305–6.

[175] W. P. W., 'Review of *Irish Witchcraft and Demonology*', pp. 85–6. This point was also raised in: MacRitchie, 'Review of *Irish Witchcraft and Demonology*', pp. 8–5.

[176] Unsigned letter to St. John D. Seymour, c.1913 (National Library of Ireland (NLI), Seymour Papers, Ms 46,866); Mrs Astell to St. John D. Seymour, 6 October 1913 (NLI, Seymour Papers, Ms 46, 866); W. Carrigan to St. John D. Seymour, 8 October 1913 (NLI, Seymour Papers, Ms 46, 866).

scholarly standards. Between the late 1930s and early 1960s, Irish history was largely concerned with political and ecclesiastical history but by the late 1960s historians became more interested in underlying economic and social structures. The following decades saw an expansion of Irish social (including medical), cultural and gender history, along with a backlash against revisionist history on the grounds that it deprived the Irish people of a national history based on popular collective memories.[177]

Irish witchcraft writing was slow to respond to historiographical trends both in Irish history and in witchcraft studies. Footnoted, historically contextualised articles about Irish witchcraft, written by professional, academic historians, Raymond Gillespie and Elwyn Lapoint, first appeared in the early 1990s. Gillespie and Lapoint's goal was to explain why there was so few trials in Ireland before decline set in after the Islandmagee trial of 1711. Their answer to this conundrum was twofold: the social and gender tensions believed to have driven accusations in Britain and Europe were lacking in Ireland; and the Gaelic-speaking, Roman Catholic, majority population did not lodge formal accusations with colonial, Protestant authorities, to which they were opposed on political and religious grounds. These readings accepted that Gaelic-Irish witchcraft was identical to Protestant belief in malefic, demonic witches.[178] Gender was first raised as an explanatory factor in Irish witchcraft accusations by Mary McAuliffe in 2009 in her micro study of the Youghal trial. McAuliffe accepted that the 1661 trial had many traits in common with English trials, as it seemingly fitted the Keith Thomas/Alan Macfarlane charity-refused model. However, McAuliffe demonstrated that part of the reason why Newton was accused, and the reason why that accusation was acted upon by local legal and clerical authorities, was because she transgressed generally accepted, moral boundaries by kissing her victims. This act of overt, female sexuality embodied the social taboo of unregulated touch and thus represented an intolerable threat to Youghal's patriarchy.[179] As has been discussed in the previous section, McAuliffe's work was closely followed, chronologically, by research which used a variety of explanatory mechanisms, including gender, to explore all aspects of Irish witchcraft and what it meant to both Protestant settlers and the Gaelic-Irish. In doing so, the

---

[177] Daly, 'State Papers', pp. 62–63; Boyce and O'Day, 'Introduction'.

[178] Lapoint, 'Irish Immunity', pp. 76–92; Gillespie, 'Women and Crime', pp. 44–7; Sneddon, 'Witchcraft Belief and Trials in Early Modern Ireland'. This question was also addressed in, Hutton, 'Witch-hunting in Celtic Societies', pp. 63–66.

[179] McAuliffe, 'Gender, History and Witchcraft', pp. 39–58. I have argued elsewhere that age conflict and the politics of reputation played an important role in this trial, which also resembled a late sixteenth-, early seventeenth-century English demonic possession/witchcraft case: Sneddon, *Witchcraft and Magic in Ireland*, pp. 79–82.

traditional chronological boundaries of early modern and modern were transgressed, and witchcraft was placed within a larger study of magical mentalities.

Conclusion

This section has shown that historical writing on Irish witchcraft writing did not
begin with St. John D. Seymour's book in 1913, or with the work of academic
historians in the 1990s. It had a far longer lineage, stretching back into the
nineteenth century. This historiography developed along different lines to that
of Britain and America in that it was written by men working outside of
academia and the standards of professional history. It also lagged behind
historiographical developments in modern Irish history. Irish witchcraft writing
was mostly light on historical contextualisation and eschewed interaction with
wider, contemporary debates on European witchcraft and witch-hunting.
Although written for the interested reader or to entertain, it was based on
primary sources previously edited and transcribed from manuscripts by antiquarians and demonologists. Collectively, Irish historiography created an
accepted narrative of Irish witchcraft centring on Irish exceptionalism which
portrayed a country largely unaffected by witchcraft belief in the medieval and
early modern periods except in the handful of exceptional cases, from the
prosecution of Alice Kyteler and her associates to the trial of Mary Butters.
This was accompanied by the notion that modern Ireland was disenchanted and
untroubled by belief in witchcraft and magic. This view of a disenchanted
Ireland was built on eighteenth-century enlightenment rhetoric that placed
distance between the rational and moderate present and irrational and religiously bigoted past. The influence of McSkimin's gendered, selective reading
of the Islandmagee trial, and of Irish witchcraft more widely, on historians,
journalists, and creative writers in the centuries after his death is difficult to
overestimate.

4 Reimagining Irish Witchcraft: Literature and the Press

This section presents a new way of looking at how gender norms and competing
views of Irish national identity were articulated and maintained in Ireland
between the late nineteenth and late twentieth centuries. An examination of
newspaper coverage of the Newton, Islandmagee, and Butters' cases[180] reveals
that journalists drew on historical writing and published primary sources when
discussing them. As a result, the Irish exceptionalism and disenchantment

---

[180] My initial study of newspaper representations of the Islandmagee witch trials conducted in 2017
paid little attention to gender or politicisation: Sneddon, 'Witchcraft Belief, Representation and
Memory', pp. 261–3.

myths propagated in historical writing are present in newspaper articles, albeit in a far more gendered and politicised way, reflecting the wider climate of political and social change. 'Faction', drama, prose, and poetry dealing with the trial of the Islandmagee have been explored to consider how writers represented witchcraft in Ireland in the late twentieth century. It is argued that even writers with the creative licence to reimagine Irish witchcraft found it difficult to completely jettison the ideological and gender baggage of earlier non-fiction writers. Through this study, Ireland is now able to be integrated into a growing body of work that examines how witchcraft and magic have been represented in literature.[181] Marion Gibson's work is particularly relevant to this study as it explores the influence of Renaissance texts on how witchcraft and witch trials were portrayed by creative writers in Britain and America between the sixteenth century and the present day.[182] Gibson argues that, 'Witchcraft depictions in fictions thus function as a cultural barometer, responding to changing pressures around authority, religion, national identity, economics, gender and sex, attitudes to past, present, and future, youth and age, science and technology, race and class and our basic understandings of human beings and nature'.[183]

Newspapers

In common with England,[184] cultural change, a rise in literacy and the expansion of the newspaper industry, saw Irish newspapers (albeit to varying degrees of regularity due to editorial policy and considerations of newsworthiness), from the mid-nineteenth century onwards, report increasingly on court cases for assault, slander, fraud, and murder that involved an accusation of witchcraft. There was more opportunity to do so because there was more crime to report on in an era of the expansion of policing and the court system. The late nineteenth century also saw a growth in numbers of Irish provincial and metropolitan newspapers and professional journalists. This occurred against the backdrop of a new mass market of Catholic and plebeian readership, increased advertising, the abolition of newspaper taxes after 1855, and innovations in printing technology, communication (telegraphy) and distribution (expansion of the railways). Operating in a period of almost continual political upheaval and turmoil, nineteenth- and early twentieth-century Irish journalists worked as recorders of these events, for a politicised press that had a long tradition of political

---

[181] Recent additions to this body of work include Szachowicz-Sempruch, 'Witch Figure in Nineteenth and Twentieth-Century Literature'; Churms, *Romanticism and Popular Magic*; Pudney, *Scepticism and Belief*.

[182] Gibson, *Rediscovering Renaissance Witchcraft*.

[183] Gibson, *Rediscovering Renaissance Witchcraft*, p. 2.

[184] Davies, 'Newspapers and Witchcraft', pp. 144–5.

engagement. From the mid-nineteenth century onwards, Irish newspapers, both provincial weeklies and Dublin dailies, were increasingly identified politically with either unionism or nationalism. Although happy to document contemporary instances of witchcraft, middle-class newspaper editors and journalists not only denied it was real but equated credulity in such matters with ignorance, backwardness, and ill education. There was no obvious anti-Catholic sub-text to this condemnation, and it appeared in newspapers of all political stamps well into the early twentieth century. Their scepticism was related in sensationalist headlines that denounced belief in witchcraft as 'scandalous', 'superstitious' and as 'folly'. Furthermore, when detailing witness testimony of believers in witchcraft, reporters often pointed out that the more educated and cultured members present in court had laughed at them. They also related the speeches and summing-up of lawyers, Justices of the Peace and Judges that mocked and/ or condemned the folly of the belief that underpinned the cases of theft, fraud or assault brought before them. Criminal cases involving witchcraft were nevertheless regarded as good copy, with broad appeal to their largely middle-class readership.[185] This culture of 'denying yet documenting the continuation of supernatural beliefs', and the marginalisation of witchcraft from mainstream culture by designating it lower-class, ignorant, rural, or foreign can also be found in America, France, and England in the nineteenth and early twentieth centuries.[186]

While the golden age of reporting criminal cases involving witchcraft was the late nineteenth century, reporting of witchcraft cases fell away in the mid-twentieth century (see section 1). However, another way in which Irish newspapers engaged with witchcraft was by detailing historic trials. These articles were mostly published in the late nineteenth and early twentieth centuries and in provincial newspapers.[187] They were, for the most part, factually accurate and based on historical work or primary sources. Newspaper coverage also bore the influence of earlier historical interpretations of Irish witchcraft belief and trials in terms of disenchantment and exceptionalism. However, Irish witchcraft was far more gendered and politicised in the hands of journalists, writing at a time

---

[185] Sneddon and Fulton, 'Witchcraft'; Sneddon, *Witchcraft and Magic in Ireland*, pp. 119–22; For more on laughter in court and it how this was reported in nineteenth-century Irish newspapers: Barclay, 'Stereotypes as Political Resistance', p. 262; Barclay, 'Singing, Performance, and Lower-Class Masculinity', pp. 746–68 (quote at pp. 746–7).

[186] Gibson, *Rediscovering Renaissance Witchcraft*, pp. 45–7 (quote at p. 46); Davies, *America Bewitched*, pp. 3–4, 11–12, 21, 128–9.

[187] This study is based on an examination of digitised newspapers published in Ireland between 1800–2014 and conducted in Autumn 2020 using the Irish Newspaper Archives and The British Newspaper Archive.

when women's roles were reformulated and their lives highly regulated, and different versions of Irish national identity were being forged.

Journalists and Historians

Factually accurate, newspaper articles on the trial of the Islandmagee witches were variously based on the contemporary pamphlet account of the trial published in 1822 by McSkimin,[188] the Tisdall letter published in 1775,[189] Classon Porter's book of 1888,[190] McSkimin's *History of Carrickfergus*,[191] and (after they were published) the *Ordnance Survey Memoirs of Ireland*.[192] Prior to 1913, and the publication Seymour's book, journalists working for the *Belfast Newsletter* found it easier to search back issues of their own newspaper for information on the Butters' trial.[193] In 1981, journalist for the *Belfast Telegraph*, Eddie McIlwaine supplemented his knowledge of the case gained while growing up in Carnmoney by consulting Revd H.J. St. J. Clarke's *Three Centuries in South-East Antrim* (Belfast, 1938), which contained a few lines on the trial.[194] After its publication, journalists used Seymour's book to write detailed and accurate accounts of the Kyteler, Newton, Islandmagee and Butters cases.[195] Journalists covering the Kyteler case on the other hand turned to the *Narrative of the Proceedings against Dame Alice Kyteler* (1843),[196] or the 1851 edition of Thomas Wrights' *Narrative of Sorcery and Magic*.[197] This evidential based approach did not prevent the *Belfast Telegraph* in November 1888 from describing the Islandmagee witches as being four in number, immediately after name-checking the 1822 pamphlet account.[198] Similarly, in November 1950, the *Northern Whig and Belfast Post* stated (erroneously) that if the second presiding Judge at the Islandmagee trial in 1711, Justice of the Court of Common Pleas, Anthony Upton, had not advised the jury against convicting the eight women they would have been 'burnt at the stake'.[199] This culture of journalists conducting their own historical research has been

---

[188] *Northern Whig*, 19 January 1885, 22 December 1911; *BT,* 15 November 1888.

[189] *Carrickfergus Advertiser*, 18 September 1896. Along with a detailed discussion of the Islandmagee trial, this issue printed, verbatim, a copy of Tisdall's letter from 1711. See also, *II*, 28 June 1966.

[190] *Belfast Evening Telegraph*, 15 November 1888.

[191] *Larne Times* (*LT*), 18 August 1928; *Ballymena Observer*, 27 January 1939.

[192] *IT*, 22 February 1999.   [193] *BNL*, 21 August 1907.   [194] *BT*, 29 September 1981.

[195] *Northern Whig*, 31 January 1921; *Holly Bough*, Christmas, 1932; *Irish Examiner*, 11 September 1969.

[196] *Southern Star*, 10 August 1935; *Eddowes's Shrewsbury Journal and Salopian Journal*, 8 November 1871.

[197] *Morning Post,* 1 April 1851.

[198] *BT*, 15 November 1888. For minor factual errors in an article about the 1698 lynching: *Dublin Weekly Nation*, 26 April 1884.

[199] *Northern Whig*, 24 November 1950.

increasingly abandoned. Present-day journalists are more likely to consult with writers and academics working on Irish witchcraft directly,[200] as part of a wider culture of academic consultancy, aided by the emphasis increasingly laid by universities on the social and cultural impact of research.[201]

Politicising Witchcraft

Recent research focusing on twentieth- and twenty-first-century Britain and America has shown that the witch figure is most prominent in culture and literature at times of national crisis, when 'radical and conservative forces are in negotiation'.[202] It is therefore unsurprising to find that witchcraft was a particularly hot topic in both Unionist and Nationalist Irish newspapers in the late nineteenth and early to mid-twentieth centuries; a period of prolonged political uncertainty and intermittent crisis and war, when the map of Ireland was redrawn and new culturally and historically informed national identities were framed. In this period, Irish journalists, following specific editorial lines, used historic witchcraft and magic cases to bolster specific views of Irish identity.

Protestant, Unionist newspapers, based in the north of the country, in common with their eighteenth-century forebears, mediated through nineteenth-century historical writing, used the Butters and Islandmagee cases to place distance between the enlightened, disenchanted present and the perceived ignorant and religiously bigoted past. As the national identity of Unionists was increasingly tied up with maintaining the Union with Britain, they quietly passed over the fact that witch trials in Ireland largely affected English and Scottish settler communities. The last thing they would have wanted to do was to intimate that Irish witchcraft was a British problem. In 1860, the *Ballymena Observer* stated that the Islandmagee witches were 'unfortunate victims of national ignorance and superstition', a barbarous time that stood in 'contrast with the light and civilisation of Ulster in the nineteenth century'.[203] In May 1929, after partition and the creation of Northern Ireland, the Protestant liberal newspaper, the *Northern Whig and Belfast Post* stated that Irish belief in witchcraft (epitomised by the Islandmagee trial) was no different from other 'superstitions' such as the belief in Banshees, fairies, and wise women.[204] In October 1931, the *Belfast Telegraph* published an article on the Mary Butters case which reprimanded 'our ancestors' for being

---

[200] *II*, 30 March 2011, 6 September 2014; *BT*, 31 March 2011, 4 November 2014.

[201] Docherty and Smith, 'Practising What We Preach?', pp. 273–80.

[202] Gibson, *Rediscovering Renaissance Witchcraft*, p. 2. See also, Gibson, 'Retelling Salem Stories', pp. 85–6.

[203] *Ballymena Observer and County Antrim Advertiser*, 24 March 1860.

[204] *Northern Whig and Belfast Post*, 4 May 1929.

'foolish' enough to believe in witchcraft.[205] In 1935, the *Northern Whig and Belfast Post* detailed the Butters case once more, remarking that although the population of Ulster no longer believed in witchcraft and magic, such 'superstition' could be 'found amongst backward people [in other countries] today'.[206] In 1963, the *Belfast Telegraph* brought contemporary butter-making expertise to bear on the case by suggesting that 'in light of modern knowledge the Mongomerys would have been better employed in keeping the dairy clean'.[207] In June 1967, the *Fermanagh Herald* reminded readers that the Islandmagee trial was illustrative of the tragedy that followed when rational people gave way to 'superstitious' beliefs such as witchcraft.[208] A couple of journalists writing in the 1930s and 1940s however bucked this trend by suggesting that was it not ignorance and irrationality that led to witch trials in Ireland but hysteria and mental illness.[209]

Newspapers whose editorial line was broadly nationalist also politicised historic witchcraft trials in a period when individual and national Irish identity was reworked and reasserted and Ireland was distanced religiously, culturally, and linguistically from the British Isles and the Imperial centre. In this reading, the morally superior, true Irish people, the Gaelic-speaking, native Irish, ensured Ireland avoided witch-hunting by not believing in witchcraft. In 1906, in a column entitled 'Fairy Stories and Legends for the Young Folks', the *Anglo-Celt* provided a strangely graphic and frank description of the 'witch mania' that swept through Europe, where witchcraft trials were 'in most cases a farce', and 'accusation practically meant conviction'. It was careful to inform its younger readers that belief in witchcraft was 'not of indigenous growth' and was imported into Ireland by the 'English colony', who in turn hosted the country's only witch trial in Kilkenny in 1324.[210] In August 1912, at the height of the Ulster crisis over the Third Home Rule Bill that would provide legislative independence or Home Rule for Ireland within the United Kingdom, the nationalist *Limerick Leader* suggested that among all European countries, Ireland was the only one to escape the 'mania' that 'caused the deaths of thousands of innocent women'. Glossing over the fact that witch-hunts also occurred in Catholic territories and states in Continental Europe, it argued that indigenous Irish 'superstitions' were 'generally harmless' and that the 'close and enlightening influence of the [Roman Catholic] clergy no doubt restrained their flocks from the exercises which were

---

205 *BT*, 31 October 1931.   206 *Northern Whig and Belfast Post*, 6 December 1935.
207 *BT*, 2 February 1963.   208 *Fermanagh Herald*, 10 June 1967.
209 *Ballymena Observer*, 27 January 1939; *LT*, 16 December 1943.
210 *Anglo-Celt*, 13 January 1906. In the early twentieth century, the *Anglo-Celt* enjoyed a large circulation in the provinces of Ulster and Leinster and possessed significant ties with the Irish Parliamentary Party (IPP). The IPP was an advocate for land reform and Home Rule: Doughan, *Voice of the Provinces*, pp. 239, 243.

committed in other countries'. The native Irish, it continued, had never
believed in witchcraft and this was why Irish witch trials (the Kyteler,
Islandmagee, and Butters cases) arose in English and Scottish colonist communities founded by immigrants from countries where witches were feared
and regularly executed.[211] In February 1922, pro-Sinn Féin, *Southern Star*
pushed the nationalist editorial line on witchcraft a step further by suggesting
that early modern, European witch-hunting had been a Protestant problem
which had only infected the Roman Catholic, Gaelic-speaking highlanders of
Scotland because of their close proximity with the Anglicised and
Anglophone, Scottish lowlands. Belief in witchcraft had on the hand 'never
found its way into native Ireland at all or disturbed Gaelic Sanity', and the
language did not possess an equivalent for the English word, 'witch'. It also
pointed to the Kyteler and Youghal trials to highlight the consequence of
letting the toxic, colonial import of witchcraft into Ireland.[212] The article
appeared as the political situation in Ireland became increasingly fraught,
coming two months after signing of the Anglo-Irish Treaty and a few months
before the start of the Irish Civil War between supporters of the Treaty, the
Provisional Government, and those who opposed it, the Irish Republican
Army (IRA). As the newly founded Irish Free State struggled to reconstruct
in the aftermath of the Civil War, the *Irish Independent* in September 1925
noted 'Ireland's clean record' and stated that the country 'fortunately, escaped
the witch fever which burned a trail through practically every village in
England and Scotland, and which has left its mark on the history of all other
countries'. The 'Irish people', it continued, had 'retained their sanity' amidst
the madness of the European witch-craze, and noted that although there were
'some few trials on charges of witchcraft in this country . . . the suspects and
their accusers were all of British blood'.[213] Thirty years later, in 1955, the
same newspaper published two articles by Malachy Hynes, who argued that
after the Kyteler trial in the fourteenth century, witchcraft was a problem that
only affected the north of Ireland, thus proving Protestants were just as
superstitious as Catholics.[214]

Gendering Witchcraft

Both the fledging Northern Ireland and the Irish Free State were particularly
concerned with regulating female behaviour and sexuality and articulating their
nationality through specific views of womanhood, emphasising purity and

---

[211] *Limerick Leader*, 5 August 1912.
[212] *Southern Star*, 18 February 1922. For more on the nationalist editorial line of the *Southern Star*
     in the 1920s: Doughan, *Voice of the Provinces*, pp. 195–6, 206–8.
[213] *II*, 14 September 1925.   [214] *II*, 28 February 1955, 3 June 1955.

innocence and roles as wives and mothers.[215] Samuel McSkimin's reading of the Islandmagee trial provided early-to-mid-twentieth-century northern journalists with a means to gender witchcraft and thus uphold hierarchical, gender norms which became particularly important to government and society in the new Northern Irish state.

The women accused of witchcraft in Islandmagee were portrayed as victims and as ideal women, pious, weak, and pliant. And any resistance they had shown to their prosecution was ignored in newspaper reports as was the existence of William Sellor. William clashed with their gendered portrayal of witches as women, and the accused women were repositioned as passive victims rather than active participants. In 1923, the *Northern Whig and Belfast Post* noted the women's industry, innocence and piety,[216] while the *Ballymena Observer* in 1939 spoke of the eight pitiable, elderly victims, 'all advanced in years'.[217] In 1943, writing for the *Larne Times*, Belfast-born, Protestant playwright and novelist, Olga Fielden, referred to the victimhood 'of the eight unfortunate women … indicted on a charge of witchcraft'.[218] In an article entitled, 'Memories of Witchcraft trials at Carrickfergus', the *Larne Times*, pointed out the Christian virtue of the women, noting that 'the accused were mostly sober, industrious people, who attended public worship, could repeat the Lord's Prayer, and had been known to pray both in public and in private, and that some of them had lately received the Communion'.[219] In this reading, which proved incredibly influential, the Islandmagee witches were robbed of the resistance and agency they had shown through the accusation and trial process. The lost-eye myth, invented by McSkimin, proved very appealing to journalists as it provided a dramatic end to a case bereft of the natural ending of execution. It also made the convicted women more worthy of readers' pity, as victims of ignorance and malice.[220] The *Northern Whig and Belfast Post* in May 1939 reinforced gender norms in a different way. It stated that if at one time Islandmagee had been 'the special home of witchcraft in the north', the 'only witchcraft suggested as existing … today is that of pretty girls, whose bright eyes make young men's hearts beat faster when glanced in their direction'.[221]

---

[215] For the Irish Free State, women and sexuality, see: Inglis, *Moral Monopoly*; Valiulis, 'Power, Gender, and Identity', pp. 117–36; Beaumont, 'Women Citizenship and Catholicism', pp. 563–85; Hug, *Politics of Sexual Morality in Ireland*; Smith, 'Politics of Sexual Knowledge', pp. - 208–33; Crowley and Kitchin, 'Producing "Decent Girls"', pp. 355–72; Luddy, 'Sex and the Single Girl in 1920s and 1930s Ireland', pp. 79–91; For Northern Ireland: Urquhart, 'Gender, Family and Sexuality, 1800–2000'; McCormick, *Regulating Sexuality*.

[216] *Northern Whig*, 10 September 1923.   [217] *Ballymena Observer*, 27 January 1939.

[218] *LT*, 16 December 1943.   [219] *LT*, 3 May 1951.

[220] *Anglo-Celt*, 1 January 1916; *LT*, 3 May 1951; *BT*, 21 March 1957.

[221] *Northern Whig and Belfast Post*, 23 May 1939.

Literature and the Trial of the Islandmagee Witches

Having outlined the pivotal role of newspapers in creating an accepted narrative of Irish witchcraft and witch trials, the remainder of the section will explore how faction, novels, poetry, and drama in the late nineteenth and twentieth centuries reinterpreted and reimagined the Islandmagee case. This work has not been analysed before, but it is crucial to our understanding of how witchcraft and witches were represented in Ireland. Excepting William Butler Yeats, Irish writers were disinterested in exceptionalism and disenchantment and with politicising Irish witchcraft. Up until the end of the twentieth century, the main way in which the influence of earlier historians and journalists came through in poems, plays and prose was in the gendered way the suspected witches were depicted. They also began to view Islandmagee itself as a place apart, positioned geographically and culturally on the edge of Northern Ireland.

Faction and Folklore

Some treatments of the Islandmagee trials straddled the border between evidence-based historical writing and creative writing. Although not referred to as faction by the authors who used it, they nevertheless blended fact and fiction and utilised the methodologies of both historical and creative writing to create works that engaged with readers but also made claims to historical truth.[222] This approach is perhaps most problematic when authors failed to inform readers that they had adopted it. Charles McConnell's short book on the Islandmagee trial, published in 2000, provides a detailed description of the trial using McSkimin's edition of the pamphlet account. The book is presented as factual history of the case but reads like a short novel. It fictionalises dialogue of witnesses, accusers, and the accused women, and invents period detail, a handful of events, and the ages, names, and back stories of characters, some real, some invented.[223] McConnell's factional account had a forerunner, which although did not go as far as he did, stretched to breaking point the limits of what the primary sources can tell us about the case. This appeared in the *Larne Times* in 1955 in an article written by W.G., entitled 'The Witches of Islandmagee' and subtitled: 'This story tells of their trial at Carrickfergus for alleged practising of witchcraft'. The 'story' was littered with factual error: it referred to the 'six' witches of Islandmagee and stated that the Mayor of Carrickfergus at the time of the trial was John Chaplain. The author's literary aspirations also took centre

---

[222] For faction and academic writing: Bruce, 'Case for Faction'.

[223] See McConnell, *Witches of Islandmagee*, pp. 2–6, 10–14, 16, 17, 28, 29, 31, 34, 35, 43, 46, 47, 51, 54, 63–65, 67.

stage, suspense was built into the narrative, and heavily descriptive prose employed: 'dark clouds which drifted like bat's wings over a wan, white moon'. With no evidentiary reason to do so, he described Dunbar's servant, Margaret Spears, as 'good-looking with jet-black hair'.[224] His readership, drawn from North Antrim, were not entirely happy with this rendering, and a few well-informed readers wrote into the newspaper to state that Dunbar was not taken to Mr James Stannus' house in Islandmagee before the trial as W.G. had claimed because Stannus had lived in Larne![225]

Yeats and Witchcraft

William Butler Yeats' *Fairy and Folk Tales of the Irish Peasantry* (1888) used the Islandmagee trial to separate Irish and British identities. Writers of the Irish Literary Revival, including Yeats, Ella Young, and (Isabella) Augusta, Lady Gregory used traditional beliefs and folklore to reassert individual and national identity and renew their connection with Ireland and new constructions of 'Irishness'. Yeats was key to the role folklore played in the Revival. He was a theorist, field-collector, and anthologist of folklore, reworking and revitalising earlier work produced by Irish Protestants, including Thomas Crofton Croker.[226] *Fairy and Folk Tales* covered a range of supernatural topics: the devil, the merrow (Irish mermaids), giants, magical healing, fairies (including changelings), and ghosts. In the chapter titled, 'Witches, Fairy Doctors', Yeats provided a range of folklore and folk tales on butter and milk-stealing witches, witch-hares, and cunning folk, taken from articles published anonymously in the *Dublin University Magazine* and *Dublin University Review*, and from the work of Letitia McClintock, Patrick Kennedy, and Jane Francesca Agnes, Lady Wilde.[227] Yeats was convinced his folkloric predecessors had captured the voice the Irish people but he selected carefully from their material, avoiding tales that were anti-Catholic, obviously moralistic, or portrayed Irish country people in a derogatory or patronising way.[228] Yeats' summary of the Islandmagee case, 'A Witch Trial', was comprised of lengthy quotations from McSkimin's *History of Carrickfergus*. Consequently, there was no mention of William Sellor, the piety and innocence of the convicted women was extolled, and the lost-eye myth recounted. As uncomfortable themes or arguments often are, 'A Witch Trial' was confined to the

---

[224] *LT*, 11 August 1955.   [225] *LT*, 13, 20 October 1955.

[226] Foster, *Words Alone*, chapter 3; For the late nineteenth, early twentieth-century Irish Revival: Brown, *Literature of Ireland*, pp. 19–21; Fitzsimmon and Murphy, *Irish Revival Reappraised*; Ó Giolláin, *Locating Irish Folklore*, p. 104.

[227] Yeats, *Fairy and Folk Tales,* pp. 149-185.

[228] Ó Giolláin, *Locating Irish Folklore*, pp. 104–5.

notes section of Yeats' book. The Islandmagee trial bore all the hallmarks of an English or a Scottish witch trial and by separating it textually from the folklore accounts of a benign, pastoral, peculiarly Irish brand of witchcraft, Yeats was able to contrast the morally superior native Irish with the witch-hunting British.[229] In his essay, 'Witches and Wizards and Irish folklore', one of two appended to Lady Gregory's two volume compilation first published in 1920, Yeats demonstrated that he was well acquainted with the history of early modern English and Scottish witchcraft trials, but intriguingly said nothing about Irish witch trials.[230]

Olga Fielden, *Witches in Eden* (1948)

After partition in 1921, producers of official publications, folklorists, ethnographers and broadcasters in Northern Ireland began to explore various aspects of Ulster identity.[231] During the Second World War, 'many Northern Irish writers adopted a regionalist ethos, and began looking to their own area to a much greater extent for cultural inspirations', while after the War 'Protestant writers such as John Hewitt, W.R. Rogers, Sam Hanna Bell and Louis MacNeice provided an alternative version of Northern Irish culture against the backdrop of, and often in contrast to, official commemoration and official literature'.[232] Part of this genre was a one-act play about the Islandmagee trial, *Witches in Eden*, written in 1948 by Olga Fielden.[233] Fielden's published play was well received by the local press in Co. Antrim,[234] and was first produced by an amateur dramatic society in March 1951, the Larne-based 'Tangent Players', for the Larne Drama Festival as 'curtain raiser' to *While the Sun Shines*, 'Terence Rattigan's sparkling comedy'.[235] It won the 'Coey Cup' award for 'one-act non-dialect plays',[236] and was made into a one-act radio play by Fielden for BBC radio in Northern Ireland a few years later.[237]

Witches in Eden was the first Irish play to have been directly based on a real witch trial, coming centuries after this had been done in England by

---

[229] Yeats, *Fairy and Folk Tales*, pp. 322-3.

[230] Gregory, *Visions and Beliefs*, pp. 247–62. For an examination of this book: Lysaght, 'Perspectives on Narrative Communication and Gender'.

[231] Harris, 'Parochial, National and Universal', pp. 304–34.

[232] McIntosh, *Force of Culture*, p. 180.

[233] Fielden, 'Witches in Eden', pp. 7–25. For the first draft of this play, which differs slightly in tone from the published version: Olga Fielden, 'Witches in Eden: A Play in One Act [1]' (Queen's University Belfast (QUB), MS 25/1/2, pp. 1–16); For O'Connor's other literary work: Phelan, 'Beyond the Pale: Neglected Northern Irish Women Playwrights', pp. 117–24.

[234] *Ballymena Observer*, 5 November 1948. [235] *LT*, 1 March 1951.

[236] *Northern Whig and Belfast Post*, 8 March 1951.

[237] Olga Fielden, 'Witches in Eden: A Short Play for the Radio (Script)', n.d. (QUB, MS 25/1/1); Doak, 'Ulster Protestant Women Authors', pp. 37–49 (p. 37); *IT*, 25 September 1973.

Thomas Dekker, John Ford and William Rowley in *The Witch of Edmonton* (1621).[238] Fielden's important play has never been studied before even though drama is increasingly recognised as an important way to understand how witchcraft was used in the past (particularly in Elizabethan, Jacobean, and Restoration England) to impart moral instruction, to bolster religious confessionalism, and shore-up established public and social order. Plays also used witchcraft to discuss race, gender, power (especially the relationships between rulers and the ruled, monarchs and subjects), and often used the categories of belief and scepticism as rhetorical tools.[239] Although Fielden's play was built on a solid bedrock of historical research, it represented a significant imaginative reworking that gendered Irish witchcraft in much the same way as McSkimin and journalists had done. It obscured William Sellor's role and ignored the accused women's agency and resistance. It went further by reducing the complex nexus of events, personalities, and wider social and cultural circumstances that underpinned the accusation and prosecution of the Islandmagee witches to a central theme of romantic jealousy and rivalry between two young women. The main accuser, Dunbar, thus betrays the perceived weaknesses of her sex, pettiness and envy, and the accused are reduced to victims of a legal system they have no control over once it is set against them. The gender politics of Fielden's play, its approach to historical accuracy, and the positioning of the witches as victims prefigure Arthur Millar's *The Crucible* (1953).

Fielden's play had an 'acting time of about 35 minutes' and was set over the course of an evening in 1711. It centred on Justice of the Peace (JP) Andrew Fergusson's investigation into Mary Dunbar's allegations that some local women had bewitched her. Having already arrested three women (Eliza Cellor, Cathy McCamont, Janet Carson) and committed them to jail to await trial, local constable Bryce Blan and Presbyterian minister, Reverend Tobias Sinclare (based on Revd Robert Sinclair), bring an old, 'drunk', blind woman, Sarah, to the Haltridge house. Dunbar had earlier reported that a woman fitting her description had used witchcraft to attack her in spirit form. Sarah is made to touch Dunbar to test if her condition worsens, and when no reaction is reported, she is dropped from the investigation. As the play progresses, Andrew Fergusson is placed in an untenable position when Dunbar accuses his wife

---

[238] For this play see, Pudney, *Scepticism and Belief*, pp. 182–208. An earlier reconstruction of the Islandmagee trial, featuring a cast of three women and four men, had been aired on BBC radio on 11 December 1937. It was scripted by Maisie Herring, using 'some old records and a contemporary account of the trial ... by Dr William Tisdall': *BNL*, 7 December 1937.

[239] Purkiss, *Witch in History*, pp. 179–271; Gibson, *Rediscovering Renaissance Witchcraft*, pp. 25–37, 44; Pudney, *Scepticism and Belief*.

and daughter, Janet Mean and Ann Fergusson. Mary's accusation of the Fergusson women is rooted in romantic jealousy as Ann once courted her fiancé, James Blythe, whom we learn only switched his affection to Dunbar upon being promised a large dowry by her uncle, James Haltridge. The play ends with the women's guilt being put beyond doubt when they are brought secretly into Dunbar's bedroom and identified not by sight but by their demonic presence. The curtain comes down to Sinclare praying on his knees for the return of Dunbar's health.[240]

The similarities between events in Co. Antrim in 1711 and the early stages of the Salem witch-hunts in Massachusetts in 1692 have been established.[241] However, close analysis of Fielden's 1948 play has uncovered its thematic and methodological connection with Millar's *The Crucible*, which was based on the Salem witch-hunt of 1692–1693. At the start of his play, Miller added a now famous caveat, 'A Note on the Historical Accuracy of this play':

> This play is not history in the sense in which the word is used by the academic historian. Dramatic purposes have sometimes required many characters to be fused into one; the number of girls involved in the 'crying-out' has been reduced; Abigail's age has been raised; while there were several judges of almost equal authority, I have symbolized them all in Hathorne and Danforth ... The fate of each character is exactly that of his historical model, and there is no one in the drama who did not play a similar – and in some cases exactly the same – role in history. As for the characters of the persons, little is known about most of them excepting what may be surmised from a few letters, the trial record, certain broadsides written at a time, and references to their conduct in sources of varying reliability. They may therefore be taken as creations of my own, drawn to the best of my ability in conformity with their known behaviour, except as indicated in the commentary I have written for this text.[242]

In an interview published in the *Saturday Review* in 1953, Miller was even more forthright in his defence of dramatic licence: 'A playwright has no debt of literalness to history. Right now I couldn't tell you which details were taken from the records verbatim and which were invented'.[243] In common with Miller, Fielden was also intimately acquainted with the primary-source material of her chosen trial. Some of her dialogue was taken directly from the depositions recorded by Mayor Edward Clements in early 1711 and first published in 1896.[244] Fielden was

[240] Fielden, 'Witches in Eden', pp. 7–25.
[241] See Sneddon, *Possessed by the Devil*, pp. 9, 44–5, 58, 50, 71, 100, 108, 170, 183.
[242] Miller, *Crucible*.   [243] Hewes, 'Broadway Postscript', p. 26.
[244] Fielden, 'Witches in Eden', p. 16: 'She'll make a picture of you, and roast it in the oven, like a lark in a pie. And then you'll die'. Compare with Deposition of John Smith of Larne, 21 March 1711 (TCD, Molyneux papers, Ms 883/2).

however as prepared as Miller to reimagine historical witchcraft. She based most of her characters on real people, including Revd Sinclare and the convicted witches, Catherine McCalmond, Elizabeth Sellor, and Janet Carson, but invented others such as Sarah and Ann Fergusson. Other real-life protagonists such as Blythe, Andrew Ferguson (written in the play as Fergusson) and Janet Main (written as Mean) were provided with new back-stories and romantic entanglements to account for their behaviour. Dunbar was not engaged to Blythe and although Janet Main was married to Andrew Ferguson, he was not a JP, and the couple did not have a daughter, Ann, who was subsequently accused of witchcraft. Mary Dunbar's exploitation of a current investigation into a witchcraft accusation to dispose of a love rival also has resonances in *The Crucible*. The political allegory contained in Miller's play that compares the Salem witch-hunts to senator Joseph McCarthy's rooting-out of 'communists' who had infiltrated the US government is well known.[245] Marion Gibson however has pointed out that it 'also contained a surprising strand of conservatism: a condemnation of feminine wiles' through Miller's 'misogynistic sexualisation' of Abigail Williams and her fictional 'attempts to dispose of John Proctor's wife Elizabeth after beginning an affair with John'.[246] The Crucible also represented a clear rejection of witch-hunters and witch-hunting and positioned witches as 'victims of tyranny and folly'.[247]

Fielden's description of a mother and daughter accused of witchcraft bore little resemblance to the dual gendered, Sellor 'witch family' comprising William Sellor, Janet Liston and Elizabeth Sellor.[248] A William Cellor is mentioned briefly in the play but he is cast as a publican supplying Sarah with sufficient alcohol that she is found 'drunk' by constable Blan, 'wi both arms round a barrel of o' beer'.[249] The Fergusson women in the play are respectable, well dressed and of a high social class. Fielden's characterisation of some of the other Islandmagee witches also conflicts with descriptions of the women found

---

[245] For cultural and literary representation of witchcraft and witch trials, in particular the Salem witch-hunts, in modern America: Rosenthal, *Salem Story*; Davies, *America Bewitched*, pp. 2, 203, 208, 223–6; Gibson, *Witchcraft Myths*; Gibson, 'Retelling Salem Stories', pp. 85–107.

[246] Gibson, *Witchcraft Myths*, p. 64.

[247] Gibson, *Rediscovering Renaissance Witchcraft*, pp. 101–2 (quote at p. 102).

[248] There are many examples of European witch trials involving a number of people from the same family (sometimes whole families): in the Basque Country in 1609, in various German territories, in the Dutch province of Drenthe, and in the Ukrainian, multi-ethnic and multi-confessional town of Vyzhva in the 1730s, which then lay in the Volhynian Palatinate of the Polish-Lithuanian Commonwealth: Briggs, *Witches and Neighbours*, p. 215; Henningsen, *Basque Witchcraft*, p. 197; Dysa, 'Family Matter', pp. 352–63; Rowlands, 'Gender, Ungodly Parents', pp. 45–86; Behringer, *Hexenverfolgung in Bayern*; De Blécourt, 'Hexenfamilien'; Willis, 'Witch Family in Elizabethan and Jacobean Print Culture', pp. 4–31.

[249] Fielden, 'Witches in Eden', p. 8.

in original documents. Janet Mean is described as a 'tall, dignified woman, richly dressed',[250] with a 'disfigured face' and an eye patch.[251] The real Janet Main was arthritic, and her face was scarred with smallpox marks. She was also described by her neighbours as an unkempt, irreligious woman with a bad temper.[252] In Fielden's play, Janet Mean, in a physical sense at least, resembles another convicted Islandmagee witch, Janet Millar, who was blind in one eye and had burns and scars on her face, having fallen in a fire.[253] Ann Fergusson, a wholly invented character, is described by Mary Dunbar in the play as passive, shrew-like, with striking eyes: 'She's wee and thin, with a piping voice like a bird. She has cruel black eyes and pouting lips.'[254]

Resistance to the prosecution process in the play is only shown by a male character, Andrew Fergusson, who is described as 'a man of forty-five, tall, dignified, and restrained, wearing the full-skirted coat of a gentleman'.[255] Fielden's Fergusson epitomises contemporary, normative masculinity and manhood: loyal and honest, he is a good father and husband, and a respectable magistrate and member of the gentry. We know very little of the real Andrew Fergusson but given the poverty of his wife it is almost certain that he was not a member of the gentry, and as such a commission as a JP would have been out of his reach. In the play, Fergusson defends the innocence of his daughter and wife in the face of Dunbar's claims and James Haltridge's accusation, and initially refuses to have them tested in the same manner as Sarah. Fergusson relents when Haltridge threatens to use the blank arrest warrant drawn-up for Sarah to arrest Janet and Ann. However, when Dunbar reacts adversely to their presence, Fergusson refuses to arrest them even although it is his professional duty to do so.[256] He comforts them by telling them that he will 'move heaven and earth to have this stopped, before it comes to trial'.[257] Near the end of the play, Fergusson tries once more to clear Janet and Ann's names by blind testing Dunbar in the hope that she will not be able to identify them. When Dunbar however senses their presence in the room, Fergusson is forced to admit that a jury will probably convict them.[258]

In Fielden's hands, the peninsula of Islandmagee is othered by the strangeness of its people, who are set apart from the rest of Ireland by their strong belief in witchcraft and magic:

REV. TOBIAS SINCLARE: They're a queer people in Islandmagee, Haltridge, You're not a man of these parts, but I am, and I'll say they're as queer a people as you'd find in the length and breadth of the land.

---

[250] Fielden, 'Witches in Eden', p. 20.   [251] Fielden, 'Witches in Eden', p. 15.

[252] McSkimin, *Islandmagee Witches*, p. 16; Sneddon, *Possessed by the Devil*, p. 15.

[253] Sneddon, *Possessed by the Devil*, p. 16.   [254] Fielden, 'Witches in Eden', p. 15.

[255] Fielden, 'Witches in Eden', p. 12.   [256] Fielden, 'Witches in Eden', pp. 15–16, 21–3.

[257] Fielden, 'Witches in Eden', p. 22.   [258] Fielden, 'Witches in Eden', p. 24.

JAMES HALTRIDGE: Don't I know it! Didn't they put spells on that white heifer of mine only last spring because I bought her over the head of John Wilson.[259]

This othering of Islandmagee can be found in an earlier short story, serialised in the *Dundalk Democrat* in 1913, by Catholic nationalist novelist and poet, Margaret T. Pender. Pender's story is set in seventeenth-century Islandmagee, which is described as a strange, desolate, bewitched land on the edge of civilisation, where 'Caura na Calligh' [Caura the hag], a Gaelic-Irish cunning woman, specialising in telling fortunes, lives in a cavern on the cliffs. It is here that Caura is apprehended and prosecuted for witchcraft by Protestant, Scottish soldiers who form part of a colonial, invading force.[260] The political overtures of Pender's story were absent from John A. Harrison's poem, 'Lines on Islandmagee, Co. Antrim', which was printed in the Unionist newspaper, *Larne Times* in 1910. For Harrison, it was not belief in magic that left the peninsula haunted but the collective memory of the trial of 'its witches', who 'still practise their arts as in days that are past', haunting the dreams and 'tales' of the 'rude, honest peasants of Islandmagee'.[261]

Reinterpreting the Islandmagee Witches

The view of the Islandmagee witches as innocent victims compliant with the male dominated legal system that condemned them was challenged in a poem written by Adrian Rice, 'Margaret Mitchell'. Rice's poem first appeared in 1990 in a box-set produced in collaboration with Irish artist Ross Wilson and titled *Muck Island*. The poem was reproduced in Rice's first full poetry collection, *The Mason's Tongue* in 1999. Rice and Wilson were intimately acquainted with the 1711 trial and with what we know about the real Margaret Mitchell. Rice's poem nevertheless chose to portray Mitchell as a single woman victimised by neighbours, while evocatively retelling the lost-eye myth. In doing so, however, he subverted traditional motifs of victimhood to suggest that it was not Margaret's compliance with patriarchy that landed her in the stocks but the threat she posed to it, by her unwomanly aggression, her magical rhymes (an inherent but feared part of her local culture), and her madness:

> *I shall go into a hare,*
> *With sorrow and sigh*
> *And mental torment.*

> Above the hill of the man of the yellow hair,
> Birds skim like stones on an ocean of air;

---

[259] Fielden, 'Witches in Eden', p. 10.

[260] M. T. Pender, 'The Irish Rapparees or the Jackets Green: A Tale of the Brave Days of Old', *Dundalk Democrat*, 27 December 1913. For Pender: *II*, 19 March 1920.

[261] *LT*, 23 July 1910.

Clouds are thick and coloured like a bruise.
And across the sloping hilltop field,
The wind runs a light green shimmer in the grass
To where he sits and shelters by the whin bushes

... sits and broods upon the times
She'd huddled against him in that spot ...
Surely not ... was she guilty of such crimes?
What secrets had she hid from him?
When did the stated sorcery begin?

Persuaded of the magic in her rhymes,
They have stood her in the Carrig stocks
And mocked her as a crazed young witch –
Hounded like the fabled lurker in the ditch.
Yet she only used the phrases that were heard
On lips around the townlands, and beyond,
And I would laugh and scorn, in my usual way,
And she would call me rude, and swear
That I could really madden her.

But there's madder than you, my love,
Though you be as mad as a March hare:
Many who will never trace
The scars of stones upon their neck
Or feel the smack of cabbage stalks
Against a reddened face.

A smurr of drifting rain
Rounded up the birds inland,
And he lifted up his hands, as if to pray,
But only breathed on them, to warm them,
Then started back for home across Drumgurland.

She lay silent in the castle hold,
As in a form, or souterrain –
Sequestered from the mind's intrigue,
The tongue's accusation,
The pishrogues of men.
Ye yarrow, yarrow, I pull thee –
And under my pillow I'll put thee
And the first young man that speaks to me
Will my own true love be.

Figure 2 'Margaret Mitchell' by Ross Wilson, 1990. Image reproduced courtesy of Adrian Rice and Ross Wilson

The first printing of the poem in 1990 was accompanied by a charcoal and pencil portrait by Wilson (Figure 2), which similarly portrayed Mitchell as a striking looking young woman. Surviving sources suggest that Mitchell was middle-aged, married to a man called 'Johnny', and came not from Islandmagee but from Kilroot, County Antrim, where Jonathan Swift had served as a Church of Ireland minister just a few years earlier. Mitchell was known as 'Mistress Ann' or 'Mrs Ann' to the other suspected witches and was charged as being one of her 'greatest tormentors'.[262]

The reimagining of the Islandmagee witches continued into the twenty-first century. An illustrated children's book, 'The last Witches of Islandmagee' (2015) tells the story of three stereotypical, 'Halloween' witches who replete with cauldrons, pointed hats, black capes, and green faces are employed by the local community in Islandmagee to use magic to protect them from a sea monster. The witches however feel they are getting too old to perform this task and employ an apprentice, 'hapless Hetty' to help them. Hetty accidently creates a magic potion that explodes and kills the monster, which has the added

---

[262] Sneddon, *Possessed by the Devil*, p. 53.

benefit of allowing the three older witches to retire to Brown's Bay in Islandmagee.[263] These likeable, elderly women who practise beneficial magic bear little or no resemblance to the real 'witches' of Islandmagee. However, in 2016, Belfast-based artist, Sarah Sheil, reimagined the Islandmagee witches in a way that did not gender Irish witches as women. 'The Revelry of Janet & Patrick Sellor', which formed part of a series of prints inspired by the 1711 trial, reintroduced a male witch, Patrick Sellor, into the public history of the case. An explanatory note on Sheil's website placed beside a digital image of the print makes it clear that Patrick is based on William Sellor. In the print, Sellor is depicted playing the fiddle, while his rebellious, wild-haired wife, Janet, dances by a foaming cooking pot.[264]

Martina Devlin's novel published in 2014, *The House Where It Happened* 'draws on a number of historical events – the Plantations of Ireland, the murder of Catholic women in 1641, and the persecution and prosecution of eight women of Islandmagee in 1711 – and weaves these together in a compelling tale of the persecution of witches in Ireland in the early eighteenth century'.[265] Although informed by McSkimin's edition of the pamphlet account, the novel contains fictious events and characters, invented ballads and historical documents, and dialogue written in an imagined historic dialect of Ulster Scots.[266] In a newspaper article in 2014, Devlin explained that one of her motivations for writing the novel was to 'give back their voices to those eight women' who 'were silenced twice: once in the courtroom, where they were disbelieved, and later being written out of history'.[267] As has been argued in this book, the Islandmagee witches were never 'written out of history', indeed, they *were* written into history in highly gendered and ideological ways. The summary of the *House Where It Happened* given on the back cover resonates with these earlier readings by linking belief in witchcraft to superstition and portraying the accused women as respectable members of their communities (my italics):

And so she [Ellen, a young servant to the Haltridge family] watches and ponders, as a seemingly normal girl [Mary Dunbar] claims she is bewitched- as a community turns against *eight respectable women*- and as malevolent forces unleashed more than half a century earlier threaten *a superstitious people'*.

This synopsis however is not entirely representative of the book. While Becky [Janet] Carson and Lizzie Cellor [Elizabeth Sellor] are described as decent, calm, and pious, Janet Liston is said to be argumentative. In keeping

---

[263] Ingram, *Last Witches*.   [264] Sarah Sheil, 'Revelry of Janet & Patrick Sellor'.

[265] Darwood, '*Review: The House Where It Happened*', p. 176.

[266] Devlin, *House Where It Happened*, pp. 3–7, 373–80.

[267] Martina Devlin, 'Witch Trials: Forgotten Women of a Bewitched Ireland', *II*, 5 September 2014.

with earlier narratives, William Cellor [Sellor] is not accused of witchcraft but matches his wife's bad temper, is fond of alcohol, and is often in trouble with the law. He does however defend his wife and daughter against the witchcraft accusations laid against them and tries to prevent them from being arrested.[268] Devlin's witches are also more than passive victims of patriarchy, and rail against the legal and community forces pitted against them, by refusing to confess and plead guilty in court: Margaret Mitchell even threatens the jury that has just convicted her of witchcraft, and when pilloried heckles the crowd until her teeth are knocked out by a stone.[269]

Conclusion

Historians working primarily in the nineteenth and early twentieth centuries created a view of Irish witchcraft belief through their discussion of historic trials (and publication of primary-source material) that shaped the work of later journalists and writers. If historians created an idea of Irish witchcraft, journalists, and writers weaponised it, and brought to a mass market. It is arguable as to how far this view would have filtered down into mainstream culture without their popularising efforts. Collectively, they created an accepted version of the history of Ireland's relationship with witchcraft, at once exceptional, disenchanted, and gendered, and in some cases tapping directly into highly politicised views of national identity. If in the twentieth century American cultural witches were used by writers to defend various positions within gender politics, from female empowerment to anti-feminism,[270] witchcraft literature in Ireland, up until the late twentieth century, reinforced traditional, patriarchal gender norms.

5 Conclusion

This Element has argued that in the two centuries that followed the repeal in 1821 of the 1586 Irish Witchcraft Act, Ireland was not disenchanted, nor did it experience a decline in magic. It has suggested that beliefs, practices, and traditions concerning witchcraft and popular magic developed and adapted to modernity to retain cultural currency up until at least the end of the twentieth century. The witch figure that emerged in the twentieth century was not as much of threat to life and limb as it had been in the previous century. In rural areas at least, witchcraft became increasingly tied up with fears over the evil eye and its threat to agricultural produce and livestock. Witchcraft accusations (or at the

---

[268] Devlin, *House Where It Happened*, pp. 124, 171–2, 184–90.
[269] Devlin, *House Where It Happened*, pp. 285–307, 330–3.
[270] Gibson, 'Retelling Salem Stories'.

very least suspicion) was less likely to lead to assault and slander (and thus court cases) as it had in the previous century, but it could still cause reputational harm and necessitate the need for protective or counter-magic. The latter half of the twentieth century saw harmful witchcraft become entangled with modern fears of Satanic witchcraft and the appearance of self-identifying witches associated with modern paganism.

This analysis of fears and beliefs surrounding witchcraft provide the backdrop to an exploration of how historic Irish trials of witches and cunning folk were represented by historians, antiquarians, journalists, dramatists, poets, and novelists, in Ireland between the late eighteenth and late twentieth centuries. It is argued that this work created an accepted narrative of Irish witchcraft and magic which glossed over, ignored, or obscured the depth of belief in witchcraft, both in the past and in contemporary society. It also gendered Irish witchcraft, created a myth of a disenchanted, modern Ireland, and reinforced competing views of Irishness and Irish identity. At a time when national identity was being refashioned and reforged in the late nineteenth and early twentieth centuries, and in the hands of a highly politicised press, this politicisation of historic trials was even more palpable. These long-held stereotypes were only challenged in the late twentieth century by historians and creative writers.

Bibliography

Published Manuscripts

McGaw, William Orr, 'Tragic Occurrence, Which Took Place in the Parish of Carnmoney and County of Antrim in the year 1807 through Belief in Witchcraft', *Ulster Journal of Archaeology*, third series, 18 (1955), 113–16.

McSkimin, Samuel (ed.), *The Islandmagee Witches: A Narrative of the Suffering of a Young Girl Called Mary Dunbar ... in the Latter End of 1710 and the Beginning of 1711* (Belfast, 1822).

Tisdall, William, 'Account of the Trial of Eight Reputed Witches, 4 April 1711', *Hibernian Magazine or Compendium of Entertaining Knowledge* (January 1775), 47–51.

Wright, Thomas (ed.), *A Contemporary Narrative of the Proceedings against Dame Alice Kyteler, Prosecuted for Sorcery in 1324 by Richard de Ledrede, Bishop of Ossory* (London: Camden Society, 1843).

Young, Robert M. (ed.), *Historical Notes of Old Belfast* (Belfast: Marcus Ward, 1896).

British Library

Western Manuscripts.

Coleraine Museum

Sam Henry Collection.

Queen's University Belfast, Special Collections

Olga Fielden, Plays and Radio Scripts.

National Archives, Kew

Royal Irish Constabulary Service Records.

National Folklore Collection, University College Dublin

The following manuscripts have been accessed via the National Folklore Collection, University College Dublin, Digitization Project, www.Duchas.ie. Main Manuscript Collection.

Photographic Collection.
Schools Folklore Scheme.

National Library of Ireland

St. John D. Seymour Papers.

Public Record Office of Northern Ireland

Benn Papers.
Ordnance Survey Memoirs, Microfilm. Originals held in Royal Irish Academy, Dublin.
Stewart Papers.
Tenant Papers.
Tyrone, Crown and Peace Records.
Young Family Papers.

Trinity College Dublin

Molyneux Papers.

Ulster Folk and Transport Museum

Collector's Notebooks.
Folklore Questionnaires.

Newspapers

Anglo-Celt.
Ballymena Observer.
Ballymena Observer and County Antrim Advertiser.
Belfast Evening Telegraph.
Belfast Morning News.
Belfast Newsletter.
Belfast Telegraph.
Caledonian Mercury.
Carrickfergus Advertiser.
Cork Examiner.
Dublin Evening Post.
Dublin Weekly Nation.
Dundalk Democrat.

Fermanagh Herald.

Hibernian Journal; or, Chronicle of Liberty.

Irish Independent.

Irish Press.

Irish Times.

Larne Times.

Limerick Leader.

Mid-Ulster Mail.

Nenagh Guardian.

Newry Reporter.

Northern Whig.

Northern Whig and Belfast Post.

Southern Star.

Westmeath Examiner.

Artwork

Sarah Sheil, 'The Revelry of Janet & Patrick Sellor' (2016). https://sarahshei lart.bigcartel.com/product/the-revelry-of-janet-patrick-sellor.

Websites

Barnard, Toby Christopher 'Seymour, St John Drelincourt', *Dictionary of Irish Biography*, www.dib.ie/biography/seymour-st-john-drelincourt-a7984.

Blúiríní Béaloidis, Folklore Podcast, 27, https://soundcloud.com/folklore_ podcast/bluirini-bealoidis-27-the-banshee-with-professor-patricia-lysaght.

McGarry, Marion, 'A Guide to Piseogs, Ireland's Sinister Folk Magic Spells', *RTÉ Brainstorm*, 6 July 2020, www.rte.ie/brainstorm/2020/0706/1151667-piseogs-ireland-folklore-evil-magic-spells/.

Thompson, Michael, 'Wright, Thomas (1810–1877), Historian and Antiquary', *Oxford Dictionary of National Biography*,www.oxforddnb.com/view/ 10.1093/ref:odnb/9780198614128.001.0001/odnb-9780198614128-e-30063.

Williams, Fionnuala Carson, 'Samuel "Sam" McSkimin, 1775–1843', *Dictionary of Irish Biography*, www.dib.ie/biography/mcskimin-samuel-sam-a5758.

Thesis

Fulton, John, 'Clerics, Conjurors and Courtrooms: Witchcraft, Magic and Religion in Eighteenth- and Nineteenth-century Ireland'. Unpublished PhD thesis, Ulster University, 2016.

Pre-1900 Publications

'A New Explanation of Old Superstitions', *Chambers's Edinburgh Journal*, 24 (1824), 382–3.

'Another Evening with the Witchfinders', *Dublin University Magazine*, 30, no. 176 (1847), 146–61.

Ady, Thomas, *A Candle in the Dark or, a Treatise Concerning the Nature of Witches and Witchcraft* (London, 1655, repr. 1656).

Croker, Thomas Crofton, 'Witchcraft in Kilkenny', *Dublin Penny Journal*, 1, no. 43 (1833), 341.

Finlay, Peter, 'Witchcraft', *Irish Monthly*, 2 (1874), 523–9.

Glanvill, Joseph, *Saducismus Triumphatus: Or, Full and Plain Evidence Concerning Witches and Apparitions* (London, 3rd ed., 1689).

McSkimin, Samuel, *The History and Antiquities of the County of the Town of Carrickfergus, Co. Antrim* (Belfast: Hugh Kirk Gordon, 1811).

McSkimin, Samuel, *The History and Antiquities of the County of the Town of Carrickfergus, Co. Antrim* (Belfast: J. Smyth, 2nd ed., 1823).

M. S. H., 'Witchcraft in Ireland', *Dublin University Magazine*, 82, no. 488 (1873), 218–23.

Porter, Classon, *Witches, Warlocks and Ghosts* (Belfast, 1885).

'Review of *Irish Witchcraft and Demonology*', *The Athenæum*, 4505 (1914), 305–6.

Scot, Reginald, *The Discoverie of Witchcraft* (London, 1584, repr. 1972).

S. M. S. [Samuel McSkimin], 'An Account of Island Magee, Taken in 1809', *Belfast Monthly Magazine*, 3, no. 13 (1809), 104–6.

S. M. S. [Samuel McSkimin], 'A Statistical Account of Island Magee', *Newry Magazine*, 3, no. 18 (1818), 506–10.

Wood, William, 'Witchcraft', *The Cornhill Magazine*, 5, no. 29 (1898), 655–70.

Wright, Thomas, *Narratives of Sorcery and Magic from the Most Authentic Sources* (New York: Redfield, 1852).

Yeats, W. B., *Fairy and Folk Tales of the Irish Peasantry* (London: Walter Scott, 1888).

Young, Robert, 'Carrickfergus', *Dublin Penny Journal*, 47, no. 1 (1833), 369–71.

Publications Post-1900

Akenson, Donald Harman, *Between Two Revolutions: Islandmagee, County Antrim, 1798–1920* (Hamden: Archon Books, 1979).

Barclay, Katie, 'Singing, Performance, and Lower-Class Masculinity in the Dublin Magistrates' Court, 1820–1850', *Journal of Social History*, 47, no. 3 (2014), 746–68. http://doi.org/10.1093/jsh/sht105.

Barclay, Katie, 'Stereotypes as Political Resistance: The Irish Police Court Columns, c.1820–1845', *Social History*, 42, no. 2 (2017), 257–80. http://doi.org/10.1080/03071022.2017.1290343.

Barnard, Toby Christopher, 'Writing and Publishing Histories in Eighteenth-Century Ireland' in Mark Williams and Stephen Paul Forrest (eds.), *Constructing the Past: Writing Irish History, 1600–1800* (Woodbridge: Boydell Press, 2010), pp. 95–112.

Barry, Jonathan, 'News from the Invisible World: The Publishing History of Tales of the Supernatural c.1660–1832' in *Cultures of Witchcraft*, pp. 179–213.

Barry, Jonathan, 'Public Infidelity and Private Belief: The Discourse of Spirits in Enlightenment Bristol' in *Beyond the Witch Trials*, pp. 117–43.

Barry, Jonathan, Owen Davies and Cornelie Usborne (eds.), *Cultures of Witchcraft in Europe from the Middle Ages to the Present* (London: Palgrave Macmillan, 2018).

Bath, Jo and John Newton, '"Sensible Proof of Spirits": Ghost Belief during the Later Seventeenth Century', *Folklore*, 117, no. 1 (2006), 1–14. http://doi.org/10.1080/00155870500479851.

Beaumont, Catriona, 'Women Citizenship and Catholicism in the Irish Free State, 1922–1948', *Women's History Review*, 6, no. 4 (1997), 563–85.

Behringer, Wolfgang, *Hexenverfolgung in Bayern: Volksmagie, Glaubenseifer und Staatsräson in der Frühen Neuzeit* (Munich: R. Oldenbourg, 1987).

Beiner, Guy, *Remembering the Year of the French: Irish Folk History and Social Memory* (London: University of Wisconsin Press, 2007).

Bell, Karl, *The Magical Imagination: Magic and Modernity in Urban England 1780–1914* (Cambridge: Cambridge University Press, 2012).

Borsje, Jacqueline, *The Celtic Evil Eye and Related Mythological Motifs in Medieval Ireland* (Leuven: Peeters, 2012).

Bourke, Angela, *The Burning of Bridget Cleary: A True Story* (London: Pimlico, 1999).

Boyce, D. George and Alan O'Day, 'Introduction' in D. George Boyce and Alan O'Day (eds.), *The Making of Modern Irish History: Revisionism and the Revisionist Controversy* (London: Routledge, 1996, repr. 1997), pp. 1–14.

Breathnach, Ciara, 'Handywomen and Birthing in Rural Ireland, 1851–1955', *Gender & History*, 28, no. 1 (2016), 34–56. http://doi.org/10.1111/1468-0424.12176.

Briggs, Robin, *Witches and Neighbours: The Social and Cultural Context of European Witchcraft* (London: Wiley-Blackwell, 2nd ed., 2002).

Briody, Mícheál, *The Irish Folklore Commission 1935–1970* (Helsinki: Finnish Literature Society, 2007).

Brown, Terence, *The Life of W. B. Yeats: A Critical Biography* (Dublin: Gill and Macmillan, 2001).

Brown, Terence, *The Literature of Ireland: Culture and Criticism* (Cambridge: Cambridge University Press, 2010).

Bruce, Toni, 'The Case for Faction as a Potent Method for Integrating Fact and Fiction in Research' in Sandy Farquhar and Esther Fitzpatrick (eds.), *Innovations in Narrative and Metaphor* (Singapore: Springer, 2019), pp. 57–72. http://doi.org/10.1007/978-981-13-6114-2_5.

Buckley, Anthony D., 'Unofficial Healing in Ulster', *Ulster Folklife*, 26 (1980), 15–34.

Butler, Alison, *Victorian Occultism and the Making of Modern Magic: Invoking Tradition* (Basingstoke: Palgrave Macmillan, 2011).

Butler, Jenny, 'The Nearest Kin of the Moon: Irish Pagan Witchcraft, Magic(k), and the Celtic Twilight' in Ethan Doyle White and Shai Feraro (eds.), *Magic and Witchery in the Modern West: Celebrating the Twentieth Anniversary of Ronald Hutton's The Triumph of the Moon* (Cham: Palgrave Macmillan, 2019), pp. 85–105.

Byrne, Patrick F., *Witchcraft in Ireland* (Dublin: Mercier Press, 1969, repr. 1973).

Callan, Maeve Brigid, *The Templars, the Witch, and the Wild Irish: Vengeance and Heresy in Medieval Ireland* (Ithaca: Cornell University Press, 2015).

Cameron, Euan, *Enchanted Europe: Superstition, Reason, and Religion, 1250–1750* (Oxford: Oxford University Press, 2010).

Cashman, Ray, 'Neighborliness and Decency, Witchcraft and Famine: Reflections on Community from Irish Folklore', *Journal of American Folklore*, 134, no. 531 (2021), 79–100.

Churms, Stephanie Elizabeth, *Romanticism and Popular Magic: Poetry and Cultures of the Occult in the 1790s* (Basingstoke: Palgrave Macmillan, 2019).

Clark, Stuart, *Thinking with Demons: The Idea of Witchcraft in Early Modern Europe* (Oxford: Oxford University Press, 1997, repr. 1999).

Cox, Catherine, 'Access and Engagement: The Medical Dispensary Service in Post-Famine Ireland' in Catherine Cox and Maria Luddy (eds.), *Cultures of*

Care in Irish Medical History, 1750–1970 (Basingstoke: Palgrave Macmillan, 2010), pp. 57–78.

Cox, Catherine, 'The Medical Marketplace and Medical Tradition in Nineteenth Century Ireland' in Ronnie Moore and Stuart McClean (eds.), *Folk Healing and Health Care Practices in Britain and Ireland: Stethoscopes, Wands and Crystals* (Oxford: Berghahn Books, 2010), pp. 55–79.

Craik, Alex, 'The Hydrostatical Works of George Sinclair (c.1630–1696): Their Neglect and Criticism', *Notes and Records: The Royal Society Journal of the History of Science*, 72 (2018), 239–73. http://doi.org/10.1098/rsnr.2017.0044.

Crone, John S., 'Witchcraft in Antrim', *Ulster Journal of Archaeology*, 14, no. 1 (1908), 34–7.

Crowley, Una and Rob Kitchin, 'Producing "Decent Girls": Governmentality and the Moral Geography of Sexual Conduct in Ireland (1922–37)', *Gender, Place and Culture*, 15, no. 4 (2008), 355–72. http://doi.org/10.1080/09663690802155553.

Curran, Bob, *A Bewitched Land: Witches and Warlocks of Ireland* (Dublin: O'Brien Press, 2005).

Daly, Mary E., '"The State Papers of a Forgotten and Neglected People"; the National Folklore Collection and the Writing of Irish History', *Béaloideas*, 78 (2010), 61–79.

Darwood, Nicola, 'Review: *The House Where It Happened*, Martina Devlin', *The Irish Journal of Gothic and Horror Studies*, 16 (2017), 175–6.

Davies, Owen, *America Bewitched: The Story of Witchcraft after Salem* (Oxford: Oxford University Press, 2013).

Davies, Owen, 'Researching Reverse Witch Trials in Nineteenth- and Early Twentieth-Century England' in *Cultures of Witchcraft*, pp. 215–32.

Davies, Owen, *The Supernatural War: Magic, Divination, and Faith* (Oxford: Oxford University Press, 2018).

Davies, Owen, *Witchcraft, Magic and Culture, 1736–1951* (Manchester: Manchester University Press, 1999).

Davies, Owen and Ceri Houlbrook, *Building Magic: Ritual and Re-enchantment in Post-medieval Structures* (Cham: Palgrave, 2021).

Davies, Owen and Francesca Matteoni, *Executing Magic in the Modern Era: Criminal Bodies and the Gallows in Popular Medicine* (Basingstoke: Palgrave Macmillan, 2017).

Davies, Owen and Willem de Blécourt (eds.), *Beyond the Witch Trials: Witchcraft and Magic in Enlightenment Europe* (Manchester: Manchester University Press, 2004).

Davies, Owen, 'Newspapers and the Popular Belief in Witchcraft and Magic in the Modern Period', *Journal of British Studies*, 37, no. 2 (1998), 139–65.

Davies, Owen and Willem de Blécourt (eds.), *Witchcraft Continued: Popular Magic in Modern Europe* (Manchester: Manchester University Press, 2004).

Day, Angélique and Patrick McWilliams (eds.), *Ordnance Survey Memoirs of Ireland* (Belfast, 40 vols, 1990–1998).

De Blécourt, Willem, 'Hexenfamilien – Zauber(er) geschlechter: Das Beispiel Drenthe (17–19 Jahrhundert)' in Eva Labouvie and Ramona Myrrhe (eds.), *Familienbande – Familienschande: Geschlechterverhältnisse in Familie und Verwandschaft* (Cologne: Böhlau-Verlag, 2007), pp. 121–45.

De Nie, Michael and Sean Farrell (eds.), *Power and Popular Culture in Modern Ireland: Essays in Honour of James S. Donnelly* (Dublin: Irish Academic Press, 2010).

Delay, Cara, *Irish Women and the Creation of Modern Catholicism, 1850–1950* (Manchester: Manchester University Press, 2019).

Dent, J. G., 'The Witch-stone in Ulster and England', *Ulster Folklife*, 10 (1964), 46–8.

Devlin, Martina, *The House Where It Happened* (Dublin: Ward River Press, 2014, repr. 2015).

Dillinger, Johannes (ed.), *The Routledge History of Witchcraft* (London: Routledge, 2020).

Doak, Naomi, 'Ulster Protestant Women Authors: Olga Fielden's Island Story', *Irish Studies Review*, 15, no. 11 (2007), 37–49.

Docherty, Iain and Denis Smith, 'Practising What We Preach? Academic Consultancy in a Multi-Disciplinary Environment', *Public Money & Management*, 27, no. 4 (2007), 273–80. http://doi.org/10.1111/j.1467-9302.2007.00594.x.

Doherty, Michael L., 'The Folklore of Cattle Diseases: A Veterinary Perspective', *Béaloideas*, 69 (2001), 41–75.

Donaldson, Dixon, *History of Islandmagee* (Islandmagee, 1927, repr. 2002).

Doughan, Christopher, *The Voice of the Provinces: The Regional Press in Revolutionary Ireland, 1914–1921* (Liverpool: Liverpool University Press, 2019).

Dowd, Marion, 'Bewitched by an Elf Dart: Fairy Archaeology, Folk Magic and Traditional Medicine in Ireland', *Cambridge Archaeological Journal*, 28, no. 3 (2018), 451–73. http://doi.org/10.1017/S0959774318000124.

Dysa, Kateryna, 'A Family Matter: The Case of a Witch Family in an Eighteenth-Century Volhynian Town', *Russian History*, 40 (2013), 352–63.

Edwards, R. W. Dudley and Mary O'Dowd, *Sources for Modern Irish History, 1534–1641* (Cambridge: Cambridge University Press, 2003).

Elmer, Peter, *The Miraculous Conformist: Valentine Greatrakes, the Body Politic, and the Politics of Healing in Restoration Britain* (Oxford: Oxford University Press, 2013).

Fexneld, Per, 'Disciples of Hell: The History of Satanism' in *Routledge History of Witchcraft*, pp. 334–48.

Fielden, Olga, 'Witches in Eden' in Patricia O'Connor (ed.), *Four New One-Act Plays* (Belfast: Quota Press, 1948), pp. 7–25.

Fitzsimmon, Betsey Taylor and James H. Murphy (eds.), *The Irish Revival Reappraised* (Dublin: Four Courts Press, 2004).

Foley, Ronan, 'Indigenous Narratives of Health: (Re)Placing Folk-Medicine within Irish Health Histories', *Journal of Medical Humanities*, 18 (2015), 5–18. http://doi.org/10.1007/s10912-014-9322-4.

Foster, Cooper Jeanne, *Ulster Folklore* (Belfast: H. R. Carter, 1951).

Foster, Roy F., *W. B. Yeats: A Life, I: The Apprentice Mage, 1865–1914* (Oxford: Oxford University Press, 1997).

Foster, Roy F., *W. B. Yeats: A Life, II: The Arch-Poet, 1915–1939* (Oxford: Oxford University Press, 2003).

Foster, Roy F., *Words Alone: Yeats and His Inheritance* (Oxford: Oxford University Press, 2011).

Garnham, Neal, 'Local Elite Creation in Early Hanoverian Ireland: The Case of the County Grand Juries', *Historical Journal*, 42, no. 33 (1999), 623–42.

Gaskill, Malcolm, *Crime and Mentalities in Early Modern England* (Cambridge: Cambridge University Press, 2000).

Gaskill, Malcolm, 'The Pursuit of Reality: Recent Research into the History of Witchcraft', *Historical Journal*, 51, no. 4 (2008), 1069–99. http://doi.org/10.1017/S0018246X0800719X.

Gaskill, Malcolm, 'Witchcraft Trials in England' in *Oxford Handbook of Witchcraft*, pp. 283–99.

Gibson, Marion, *Rediscovering Renaissance Witchcraft: Witches in Early Modernity and Modernity* (Abingdon: Routledge, 2018).

Gibson, Marion, 'Retelling Salem Stories: Gender Politics and Witches', *American Culture European Journal of American Culture*, 25, no. 2 (2006), 85–107.

Gibson, Marion, *Witchcraft: The Basics* (Abingdon: Routledge, 2018).

Gibson, Marion, *Witchcraft Myths in American Culture* (Abingdon: Routledge, 2007).

Gillespie, Raymond, 'Women and Crime in Seventeenth-Century Ireland' in Margaret MacCurtain and Mary O'Dowd (eds.), *Women in Early Modern Ireland* (Edinburgh: Edinburgh University Press, 1991), pp. 43–52.

Gillespie, Raymond and Andrew Hadfield (eds.), *The Oxford History of the Irish Book: Volume III, The Irish Book in English, 1550–1800* (Oxford: Oxford University Press, 2006).

Glassie, Henry, *Passing the Time in Ballymenone: History and Culture of an Ulster Community* (Bloomington: Indiana University Press, 1995).

Goodare, Julian, *The European Witch-hunt* (Abingdon: Routledge, 2016).

Gregory, Lady, *Visions and Beliefs in the West of Ireland Collected and Arranged by Lady Gregory: With Two Essays and Notes by W. B. Yeats* (New York: Knickerbocker Press, 1920).

Gribben, Crawford, *The Rise and Fall of Christian Ireland* (Oxford: Oxford University Press, 2021).

Hall, Wayne E., *Dialogues in the Margin: A Study of the Dublin University Magazine* (Buckinghamshire: Colin Smythe, 2000).

Harper, George Mills (ed.), *Yeats and the Occult* (Basingstoke: Macmillan, 1976).

Harris, Mary N., 'Parochial, National and Universal: The Concerns of Irish Regional Publishing' in Clare Hutton and Patrick Walsh (eds.), *The Irish Book in English, 1891–2000* (Oxford: Oxford University Press, 2011), pp. 304–34.

Hayton, David, *Ruling Ireland, 1685–1742: Politics, Politicians and Parties* (Suffolk: Boydell Press, 2004).

Henderson, Lizanne, *Witchcraft and Folk Belief in the Age of Enlightenment: Scotland, 1670–1740* (Basingstoke: Palgrave Macmillan, 2016).

Henningsen, Gustav, *The Witches' Advocate: Basque Witchcraft and the Spanish Inquisition, 1609–1614* (Reno: University of Nevada Press, 1980).

Hewes, Henry, 'Broadway Postscript: Arthur Miller and How He Went to the Devil', *Saturday Review* (21 January 1953), p. 26.

Houlbrook, Ceri and Natalie Armitage (eds.), *The Materiality of Magic* (Oxford: Oxbow Books, 2015).

Hug, Crystal, *The Politics of Sexual Morality in Ireland* (Basingstoke: Palgrave, 1999).

Hunter, Michael, *The Decline of Magic: Britain in the Enlightenment* (New Haven: Yale University Press, 2020).

Hutton, Ronald (ed.), *Physical Evidence for Ritual Acts, Sorcery and Witchcraft in Christian Britain* (Basingstoke: Palgrave Macmillan, 2016).

Hutton, Ronald, 'The Changing Face of Manx Witchcraft', *Cultural and Social History*, 7, no. 22 (2010), 153–69. http://doi.org/10.2752/147800410X12634795054531.

Hutton, Ronald, *The Triumph of the Moon: A History of Modern Pagan Witchcraft* (Oxford: Oxford University Press, 1999).

Hutton, Ronald, *The Witch: A History of Fear, from Ancient Times to the Present* (New Haven: Yale University Press, 2017).

Hutton, Ronald, 'Witch-hunting in Celtic Societies', *Past and Present*, 212, no. 1 (2011), 43–71. http://doi.org/10.1093/pastj/gtr003.

Inglis, Tom, *Moral Monopoly: The Rise and Fall of the Catholic Church in Modern Irish Society* (Dublin: University College Dublin Press, 1987).

Ingram, Luan, *The Last Witches of Islandmagee* (Kraken, 2015).

Irwin, Liam, 'Thomas Johnston Westropp, 1860–1922' in Próinséas Ní Chatháin, Siobhán Fitzpatrick and Howard Clarke (eds.), *Pathfinders to the Past: The Antiquarian Road to Irish Historical Writing, 1640–1960* (Dublin: Four Courts Press, 2012), pp. 131–43.

I. P., 'On the Rise and Progress of Witchcraft, no. III', *The Gentleman's Magazine and Historical Chronicle* (1829), pp. 580–5.

Jenkins, Richard, *Black Magic and Bogeymen: Fear, Rumour and Popular Belief in the North of Ireland, 1972–4* (Cork: Cork University Press, 2014).

Jenkins, Richard, 'Disenchantment, Enchantment and Re-Enchantment: Max Weber at the Millennium', *Max Weber Studies*, 1, no. 1 (2000), 11–32.

Jenkins, Richard, 'Spooks and Spooks: Black Magic and Bogeymen in Northern Ireland, 1973–4' in *Witchcraft Continued*, pp. 191–212.

Jenkins, Richard, 'The Transformations of Biddy Early: From Local Reports of Magical Healing to Globalised New Age Fantasy', *Folklore*, 118, no. 2 (2007), 162–82. http://doi.org/10.1080/00155870701337379.

La Fontaine, Jean, 'Satanism and Satanic Mythology' in Willem de Blécourt, Ronald Hutton and Jean La Fontaine (eds.), *The Athlone History of Witchcraft and Magic in Europe: The Twentieth Century* (London: Athlone Press, 1999), pp. 83–140.

Lapoint, Elwyn C., 'Irish Immunity to Witch-Hunting, 1534–1711', *Eire Ireland*, 27, no. 2 (1992), 76–92.

Larner, Christina, *Enemies of God: The Witch-hunt in Scotland* (London: Chatto and Windus, 1981).

Leeder, Murray, *The Modern Supernatural and the Beginnings of Cinema* (Basingstoke: Palgrave Macmillan, 2017).

Lehane, Shane, 'The Cailleach and the Cosmic Hare' in Barbara Hillers, Ciarán Ó Gealbháin, Ilona Tuomi and John Carey (eds.), *Charms, Charmers and Charming in Ireland: From the Medieval to the Modern* (Melksham: University of Wales Press, 2019), pp. 189–204.

Levack, Brian (ed.), *The Oxford Handbook of Witchcraft in Early Modern Europe and Colonial America* (Oxford: Oxford University Press, 2013).

Linn, Meredith B., 'Irish Immigrant Healing Magic in Nineteenth-Century New York City', *Historical Archaeology*, 48, no. 3 (2014), 144–65.

Luddy, Maria, 'Sex and the Single Girl in 1920s and 1930s Ireland', *The Irish Review*, 35 (2007), 79–91.

Lysaght, Patricia, 'Perspectives on Narrative Communication and Gender: Lady Augusta Gregory's Visions and Beliefs in the West of Ireland (1920)', *Fabula*, 39, no. 3–4 (1998), 256–76.

Lysaght, Patricia, *The Banshee: The Irish Supernatural Death Messenger* (Dublin: O'Brien Press, 1986).

Mac Cárthaigh, Críostóir, 'The Ship-Sinking Witch: A Maritime Folk Legend from North-West Europe', *Béaloideas*, 60/61 (1992), 267–86. http://doi.org/10.2307/20522410.

MacCarthy, B. G., 'Thomas Crofton Croker 1798–1854', *Studies: An Irish Quarterly Review*, 32, no. 128 (1943), 539–56.

MacCartney, Donald, 'The Writing of History in Ireland 1800–30', *Irish Historical Studies*, 10, no. 40 (1957), 347–62.

Machielsen, Jan, *The War on Witchcraft: Andrew Dickson White, George Lincoln Burr, and the Origins of Witchcraft Historiography* (Cambridge: Cambridge University Press, 2021).

MacRitchie, David, 'Review of *Irish Witchcraft and Demonology*', *The Celtic Review*, 10, no. 37 (1914), 8–5.

Martin, Lauren, 'Witchcraft and Family: What can Witchcraft Documents Tells Us about Early Modern Scottish Family Life?', *Scottish Tradition*, 27 (2002), 7–22. http://doi.org/10.21083/irss.v27i0.195.

McAuliffe, Mary, 'Gender, History and Witchcraft in Early Modern Ireland: A Re-reading of the Florence Newton Trial' in Mary Ann Gialenella Valiulis (ed.), *Gender and Power in Irish History* (Dublin: Irish Academic Press, 2009), pp. 39–58.

McConnell, Charles, *The Witches of Islandmagee* (Carrickfergus: Carmac Books, 2000).

McCormick, Leanne, *Regulating Sexuality: Women in Twentieth Century Northern Ireland* (Manchester: Manchester University Press, 2009).

McCrum, Elizabeth J. (ed.), *The History and Antiquities of the County of the Town of Carrickfergus by Samuel McSkimin* (Belfast: Mullan & Son, James Cleeland, Davidson, and McCormack, 1909).

McDonough, Ciaran, 'Folk Belief and Landscape in Connacht: Accounts from the Ordnance Survey letters', *Folk Life*, 57, no. 1 (2019), 56–69.

McGarry, Marion, *Irish Customs and Rituals: How Our Ancestors Celebrated Life and the Seasons* (Dublin: Orpen Press, 2020).

McGaw, William Orr, 'Notes on the Parish of Carnmoney, Co. Antrim', *Ulster Folklife*, 1 (1955), 53–7.

McIntosh, Gillian, *The Force of Culture: Unionist Identities in Twentieth-Century Ireland* (Cork: Cork University Press, 1999).

Melechi, Antonio, *Servants of the Supernatural: The Night Side of the Victorian Mind* (London: Arrow Books, 2009).

Merrifield, Ralph, *The Archaeology of Ritual and Magic* (London: New Amsterdam Books, 1987).

Meyer, Birgit and Peter Pels (eds.), *Magic and Modernity: Interfaces of Revelation and Concealment* (Stanford: Stanford University Press, 2003).

Miller, Arthur, *The Crucible: A Play in Four Acts* (London: Penguin, 1953, repr. 2000).

Monod, Paul Kléber, *Solomon's Secret Arts: The Occult in the Age of Enlightenment* (New Haven: Yale University Press, 2013).

Moore, Ronnie, 'A General Practice, a Country Practice: The Cure, the Charm and Informal Healing in Northern Ireland' in Ronnie Moore and Stuart McClean (ed.), *Folk Healing and Health Care Practices in Britain and Ireland: Stethoscopes, Wands and Crystals* (Oxford: Berghahn Books, 2010), pp. 104–29.

Moutray Read, D. H., 'Review of *Irish Witchcraft and Demonology*', *Folklore*, 27, no. 3 (1916), 322–3.

Murphy, James H. (ed.), *The Oxford History of the Irish Book: Volume IV, The Irish Book in English, 1800–1891* (Oxford: Oxford University Press, 2011).

Murphy, Michael J., *Rathlin: Island of Blood and Enchantment* (Dundalk: Dundalgan Press, 1987).

Nildin-Wall, Bodil and Jan Wall, 'The Witch as Hare or the Witch's Hare: Popular Legends and Beliefs in Nordic Tradition', *Folklore*, 104, no. 1–2 (1993), 67–76. http://doi.org/10.1080/0015587X.1993.9715854.

Ó Crualaoich, Gearóid, *The Book of the Cailleach: Stories of the Wise-Woman Healer* (Cork: Cork University Press, 2003, repr. 2015).

Ó Giolláin, Diarmuid, *Locating Irish Folklore: Tradition, Modernity, Identity* (Cork: Cork University Press, 2000, repr. 2004).

Ó Muirithe, Diarmaid and Deirdre Nuttall (eds.), *Folklore of County Wexford* (Dublin: Four Courts Press, 1999).

Owen, Alex, *The Darkened Room: Women, Power and Spiritualism in Late Victorian England* (London: Virago Press, 1989).

Owen, Alex, *The Place of Enchantment: British Occultism and the Culture of the Modern* (Chicago: University of Chicago Press, 2004).

Paterson, T. G. F., *County Cracks: Old Tales from the County of Armagh* (Dundalk: Dundalgan Press, 1945).

Pels, Peter, 'Introduction: Magic and Modernity' in *Magic and Modernity*, pp. 1–38.

Phelan, Mark, 'Beyond the Pale: Neglected Northern Irish Women Playwrights, Alice Milligan, Helen Waddell and Patricia O'Connor' in Melissa Sihra (ed.), *Women in Irish Drama: A Century of Authorship and Representation* (Basingstoke: Palgrave, 2007), pp. 109–29.

Pudney, Eric, *Scepticism and Belief in English Witchcraft Drama, 1538–1681* (Lund: Lund University Press, 2019).

Purkiss, Diane, *The Witch in History: Early Modern and Twentieth-Century Representations* (London: Routledge, 1996).

Rice, Adrian, *The Mason's Tongue* (Belfast: Abbey Press, 1999).

Riddell, William Renwick, 'The First Execution for Witchcraft in Ireland', *Journal of the American Institute for Criminal Law and Criminology*, 7, no. 6 (1917), 828–37.

Riordan, Michael, 'Materials for History? Publishing Records as a Historical Practice in Eighteenth and Nineteenth-Century England', *History of Humanities*, 2, no. 1 (2017), 51–77. http://doi.org/10.1086/690572.

Roper, Lyndal, *Witch Craze: Terror and Fantasy in Baroque Germany* (New Haven: Yale University Press, 2004).

Rosenthal, Bernard, *Salem Story: Reading the Witch Trials of 1692* (Cambridge: Cambridge University Press, 1993, repr. 1995).

Rowlands, Alison, 'Gender, Ungodly Parents, and a "Witch Family" in Seventeenth-Century Germany', *Past and Present*, 232, no. 1 (2016), 45–86. http://doi.org/10.1093/pastj/gtw014.

Saler, Michael, 'Modernity and Enchantment: A Historiographic Review', *The American Historical Review*, 111, no. 3 (June 2006), 692–716. http://doi.org/10.1086/ahr.111.3.692.

Seymour, St John D., *Irish Witchcraft and Demonology* (Dublin: Hodges, Figgis, 1913, repr. 1989).

Sharpe, James, 'Witch-hunting and Witch Historiography: Some Anglo-Scottish Comparisons' in Julian Goodare (ed.), *The Scottish Witch-hunt in Context* (Manchester: Manchester University Press, 2002), pp. 182-97.

Smith, James M., 'The Politics of Sexual Knowledge: The Origins of Ireland's Containment Culture and the Carrigan Report (1931)', *Journal of the History of Sexuality*, 13, no. 2 (2004), 208–33.

Sneddon, Andrew, 'Gender, Folklore and Magical Healing in Ireland, 1852–1922' in Jyoti Atwal, Ciara Breathnach and Sarah Ann Buckley (eds.), *Gender and History: Ireland 1852–1922* (Routledge India, forthcoming).

Sneddon, Andrew, 'Medicine, Belief, Witchcraft and Demonic Possession in Late Seventeenth-Century Ulster', *Medical Humanities*, 42 (2016), 81–6. http://doi.org/10.1136/medhum-2015-010830.

Sneddon, Andrew, *Witchcraft and Magic in Ireland* (Basingstoke: Palgrave Macmillan, 2015).

Sneddon, Andrew, *Possessed by the Devil: The Real History of the Islandmagee Witches & Ireland's Only Witchcraft Mass Trial* (Dublin: History Press Ireland, 2013).

Sneddon, Andrew, 'Select Document: Florence Newton's Trial for Witchcraft, Cork, 1661: Sir William Aston's Transcript', *Irish Historical Studies*, 43, no. 164 (2019), 298–319. http://doi.org/10.1017/ihs.2019.55.

Sneddon, Andrew, 'The Templars, the Witch, and the Wild Irish: Vengeance and Heresy in Medieval Ireland by Maeve Brigid Callan (Review)', *Magic, Ritual, and Witchcraft*, 12, no. 11 (2017), 139–42.

Sneddon, Andrew, 'Witchcraft Belief, Representation and Memory in Modern Ireland', *Cultural and Social History*, 16, no. 3 (2019), 251–70. http://doi.org/10.1080/14780038.2019.1595273.

Sneddon, Andrew, 'Witchcraft Belief and Trials in Early Modern Ireland', *Irish Economic and Social History*, 39, no. 1 (2012), 1–25.

Sneddon, Andrew and John Fulton, 'Witchcraft, the Press and Crime in Ireland, 1822–1922', *Historical Journal*, 62, no. 3 (2019), 741–64. http://doi.org/10.1017/S0018246X18000365.

Storm, Jason Ānanda Josephson, *The Myth of Disenchantment: Magic, Modernity, and the Birth of the Human Sciences* (Chicago: University of Chicago Press, 2017).

Suggett, Richard, *A History of Magic and Witchcraft in Wales* (Stroud: History Press, 2008).

Summers, Montague, *The History of Witchcraft and Demonology* (London: Kegan Paul, 1926).

Szachowicz-Sempruch, Justyna, 'The Witch Figure in Nineteenth and Twentieth-Century Literature' in *Routledge History of Witchcraft*, pp. 370–81.

Tait, Clodagh, 'Worry Work: The Supernatural Labours of Living and Dead Mothers in Irish Folklore', *Past and Present*, 246, Issue Supplement 15 (2020), 217–38. http://doi.org/10.1093/pastj/gtaa042.

Tallis, Lisa Mari, 'Which Craft? Witches, Gypsies, and the Fenyw Hysbys in Eighteenth-Century Wales', *Preternature: Critical and Historical Studies on the Preternatural*, 8, no. 2 (2019), 231–53.

Taussig, Michael, 'Viscerality, Faith and Scepticism: Another Theory of Magic' in *Magic and Modernity*, pp. 272–306.

Tilley, Elizabeth, 'Periodicals' in *Oxford History of the Irish Book: Volume IV*, pp. 144–73.

Underwood, E. Ashworth, 'Dr. J. D. Rolleston', *Nature*, 157 (1946), 506. http://doi.org/10.1038/157506a0.

Urquhart, Diane, 'Gender, Family and Sexuality, 1800–2000' in Liam Kennedy and Philip Ollerenshaw (eds.), *Ulster since 1600: Politics, Economy and Society* (Oxford: Oxford University Press, 2013), pp. 245–59.

Valiulis, Maryann Gialanella, 'Power, Gender, and Identity in the Irish Free State', *Journal of Women's History*, 7, no. 1 (1995), 117–36. http://doi.org/10.1080/09612025.2011.599612.

Walsham, Alexandra, 'The Reformation and "the Disenchantment of the World" Reassessed', *Historical Journal*, 51, no. 2 (2008), 497–528. http://doi.org/10.1017/S0018246X08006808.

Waters, Thomas, *Cursed Britain: A History of Witchcraft and Black Magic in Modern Times* (New Haven: Yale University Press, 2019).

Waters, Thomas, 'Irish Cursing and the Art of Magic, 1750–2018', *Past and Present*, 247, no. 1 (May 2020), 113–49. http://doi.org/10.1093/pastj/gtz051.

Waters, Thomas, 'Maleficent Witchcraft in Britain since 1900', *History Workshop*, 80, no. 1 (2015), 99–122. http://doi.org/10.1093/hwj/dbv014.

Waters, Tom, 'Belief in Witchcraft in Oxfordshire and Warwickshire, c. 1860–1900: The Evidence of the Newspaper Archive', *Midland History*, 34, no. 1 (2009), 98–116. http://doi.org/10.1179/175638109X406640.

Westropp, Thomas Johnson, 'A Study of the Folklore on the Coasts of Connacht, Ireland (Continued)', *Folklore*, 33, no. 4 (1922), 389–97.

Willis, Deborah, 'The Witch Family in Elizabethan and Jacobean Print Culture', *Journal of Early Modern Cultural Studies*, 13, no. 1 (2013), 4–31.

Winter, Alison, *Mesmerised: Powers of Mind in Victorian Britain* (Chicago: University of Chicago, 1998).

Wolf, Nicholas, 'Orthaí and Orthodoxy: Healing Charms in Irish Popular Religion' in *Power and Popular Culture in Modern Ireland*, pp. 125–44.

W. P. W., 'Review of *Irish Witchcraft and Demonology*', *Irish Church Quarterly*, 7, no. 25 (1914), 85–6.

Acknowledgements

I want to thank staff and students in history at Ulster University and my research director, Professor Ian Thatcher, for a period of research leave that allowed me to finish this book. I would also like to thank colleagues in the *Ulster Society for Irish Historical Studies* for allowing me to be their president for the last six years, and for the privilege of chairing some of the best new scholarship in Irish history. I would also like to thank Roger Dixon of the Ulster Folk and Transport Museum for our chats over the years about Irish folklore and the collections that he looked after for many years as librarian. I would also like to thank friends and colleagues at the Public Record Office of Northern Ireland (especially Janet Hancock, Graham Jackson and Stephen Scarth) for allowing me to access to their wonderful collections and help organise several spooky events on ghosts and witches. I have also benefitted from long chats and shared projects with various colleagues and friends: Dr Ciara Breathnach, Dr Katherine Byrne, Professor Owen Davies, Dr Elaine Farrell, Dr Frank Ferguson, Dr Helen Jackson, Dr Elizabeth Kiely, Dr Jan Machielsen, Dr Charlotte-Rose Millar, Dr Victoria McCollum, Dr John Privilege, Professor Diane Purkiss, Adrian Rice, Sarah Sheil, Dr Lisa Tallis, Dr James Ward, Dr Thomas Waters, and Dr Nerys Young. Special thanks go to Professor Marion Gibson for being so understanding and supportive throughout the publishing process. Thanks also to Sharon, Steve, and Pippa Reid for all their support, and to Vivian and Jim McCormick my parents-in-law. I want to thank my children, Andrew, and James, for coping with a father, who over the last year has been even more buried in books and paper than usual. Finally, I want to thank my wife, Dr Leanne McCormick for all the help she has provided over the years. She is a brilliant historian, and without her, my work would be much worse; as ever her exceptional insight and comments have been invaluable.

For Sharon, Steve, and Pippa Reid

Cambridge Elements ≡

Magic

Marion Gibson
University of Exeter

Marion Gibson is Professor of Renaissance and Magical Literatures and Director of the Flexible Combined Honours Programme at the University of Exeter. Her publications include *Possession, Puritanism and Print: Darrell, Harsnett, Shakespeare and the Elizabethan Exorcism Controversy* (2006), *Witchcraft Myths in American Culture* (2007), *Imagining the Pagan Past: Gods and Goddesses in Literature and History since the Dark Ages* (2013), *The Arden Shakespeare Dictionary of Shakespeare's Demonology* (with Jo Esra, 2014), *Rediscovering Renaissance Witchcraft* (2017) and *Witchcraft: The Basics* (2018). Her new book, *The Witches of St Osyth: Persecution, Murder and Betrayal in Elizabethan England*, will be published by CUP in 2022.

About the Series

Elements in Magic aims to restore the study of magic, broadly defined, to a central place within culture: one which it occupied for many centuries before being set apart by changing discourses of rationality and meaning. Understood as a continuing and potent force within global civilisation, magical thinking is imaginatively approached here as a cluster of activities, attitudes, beliefs and motivations which include topics such as alchemy, astrology, divination, exorcism, the fantastical, folklore, haunting, supernatural creatures, necromancy, ritual, spirit possession and witchcraft.

Cambridge Elements ☰

Magic

Elements in the Series

Printed in the United States
by Baker & Taylor Publisher Services